Gerald V. Miller, PhD

The Gay Male's Odyssey in the Corporate World: From Disempowerment to Empowerment

*Pre-publication
REVIEWS,
COMMENTARIES,
EVALUATIONS . . .*

"This groundbreaking work is addressed to gay males in America's 'last great closet,' the corporate world. Two other groups also will benefit from Miller's important study: (1) heterosexual executives and policy makers who are committed to transforming their corporations into centers where productivity and diversity go hand in hand, plus (2) consultants and trainers who are hired to help them do so. Informed by the author's own heroic journey of empowerment, the book is also based on questionnaire responses of two-hundred gay male managers and executives ranging from first level supervisors to executive vice presidents, and the intimate stories of forty gay male executives who are

out of the closet at work. Painstakingly documented and presented with the precision of a social scientist, the work describes what corporate life is like for most gay managers. By peeling off the self-protective skin of denial, it allows the reader to see what goes on in the minds, hearts, and guts of those who decide to take charge of their own lives, become visible, and claim their gay identity within the corporate world. Carefully data-based and academically rooted, it is inspired by the author's passionate sense of mission, which is epitomized in one sentence: 'Playing it safe is the most dangerous thing you can do.'"

Donald C. Klein, PhD
Core Faculty Member,
The Union Institute,
Cincinnati, Ohio

Harrington Park Press
An Imprint of The Haworth Press, Inc.

The Gay Male's Odyssey in the Corporate World

*From Disempowerment
to Empowerment*

HAWORTH Gay and Lesbian Studies
John P. De Cecco, PhD
Editor in Chief

New, Recent, and Forthcoming Titles:

Gay Relationships edited by John De Cecco

Perverts by Official Order: The Campaign Against Homosexuals by the United States Navy by Lawrence R. Murphy

Bad Boys and Tough Tattoos: A Social History of the Tattoo with Gangs, Sailors, and Street-Corner Punks by Samuel M. Steward

Growing Up Gay in the South: Race, Gender, and Journeys of the Spirit by James T. Sears

Homosexuality and Sexuality: Dialogues of the Sexual Revolution, Volume I by Lawrence D. Mass

Homosexuality as Behavior and Identity: Dialogues of the Sexual Revolution, Volume II by Lawrence D. Mass

Sexuality and Eroticism Among Males in Moslem Societies edited by Arno Schmitt and Jehoeda Sofer

Understanding the Male Hustler by Samuel M. Steward

Men Who Beat the Men Who Love Them: Battered Gay Men and Domestic Violence by David Island and Patrick Letellier

The Golden Boy by James Melson

The Second Plague of Europe: AIDS Prevention and Sexual Transmission Among Men in Western Europe by Michael Pollak

Barrack Buddies and Soldier Lovers: Dialogues with Gay Young Men in the U.S. Military by Steven Zeeland

Outing: Shattering the Conspiracy of Silence by Warren Johansson and William A. Percy

The Bisexual Option by Fritz Klein

And the Flag Was Still There: Straight People, Gay People, and Sexuality in the U.S. Military by Lois Shawver

One-Handed Histories: The Eroto-Politics of Gay Male Video Pornography by John R. Burger

Sailors and Sexual Identity: Crossing the Line Between "Straight" and "Gay' in the U.S. Navy by Steven Zeeland

The Gay Male's Odyssey in the Corporate World: From Disempowerment to Empowerment by Gerald V. Miller

Bisexual Politics: Theories, Queries, and Visions by Naomi Tucker

The Gay Male's Odyssey in the Corporate World
From Disempowerment to Empowerment

Gerald V. Miller, PhD

Harrington Park Press
An Imprint of The Haworth Press, Inc.
New York • London

Published by

Harrington Park Press, an imprint of The Haworth Press, Inc., 10 Alice Street, Binghamton, NY 13904-1580

The Haworth Press, Inc., 10 Alice Street, Binghamton, NY 13904-1580

Library of Congress Cataloging-in-Publication Data

Miller, Gerald V.
    The gay male's odyssey in the corporate world: From disempowerment to empowerment / Gerald V. Miller.
        p.   cm.
    Includes bibliographical references and index.
    ISBN 1-56023-867-4
    1. Gay men–Employment. 2. Corporate culture. I. Title.
HD6285.M55 1994
331.5–dc20

94-47539
CIP

Dedicated to James T. Russler

1949-1992

My best and longest friend,
without your constant patience,
love, and support this work
could not have been started
in your physical presence and completed
with your spiritual guidance.

By which men grow immortal; know this too:
I am so grateful, that while I breathe air
My tongue shall speak the thanks which
are your due.
Dante Alighieri

ABOUT THE AUTHOR

Gerald V. Miller, PhD, an organizational and clinical psychologist, management consultant, trainer, lecturer, and author, is President and Owner of Gerald V. Miller Associates, Inc. This Association provides quality management and organization consulting and training, as well as human resource development services, and has a clientele from both public and private sectors, including AT&T and the U.S. Department of Labor. Dr. Miller is a specialist in clinical and organizational psychology with over 20 years of experience and is a member of the American Psychological Association and the National Association of Social Workers.

CONTENTS

Acknowledgments

This book is the product of an almost lifelong odyssey. There is no way I can list all those superb human beings who held my hand, directed me, cheered me on, and accompanied me on this sojourn. However, many stand out and deserve not only recognition and acknowledgment but my profound and deepest gratitude.

I owe much to James Russler for giving me support, energy, insight, and assistance in every phase of this book. In his memory this book is dedicated.

Mr. Larry Kulp was crucial to my effort. Without his understanding and patience these pages would not have been so expertly and creatively illustrated and formatted.

Special thanks to Douglas Harrington, whose reader's eyes eliminated ambiguity and clarified the work.

Unfairly, one person will get the credit for whatever is of value within these pages. However, many have contributed to them. To all of them I owe my sincere appreciation, not only for their time, technical expertise, and residue of wisdom, but more so for the spirit of love in which the help was given.

My greatest appreciation goes to the gay men who volunteered to share their struggles and visions. Without their trust and candor, there would be no book.

Chapter 1

The Need for the Journey

The sole purpose of human existence is to kindle a light in the darkness of mere being.

–Carl Jung

Work and sexuality are not distinct species. An asexual work environment does not exist. To believe otherwise is to fall into the impervious "sexuality doesn't matter" trap.

Being gay is an issue and in most cases it is perceived as a deficiency, as verified by the research that supports this study.

Homosexuality becomes a conceptual stand, by organizational leaders and members. The stand is: being gay equals, by and large, professional incompetency, even when concrete data show that gays tend to be overachievers (Zoglin, 1979).

One's sex life, heterosexual or homosexual, is private. One's sexuality is relevant to work. When one places a picture of the spouse and children on his desk he is "coming out" as a heterosexual. Those who state that personal knowledge about sexuality is not relevant to their professional work are living an illusion. Those who state that they should be judged *only* on the quality of their work are living an illusion. At the risk of using a double negative, one cannot not make a statement about one's sexuality. To not place a picture on one's desk is to make a sexual statement.

One premise of this book, therefore, is that sexuality and work are not separate. The minority, different position of gays, therefore, requires a journey from disempowerment to empowerment. Given this reality, what are the choices?

Although this study's unit of analysis is gay males in business organizations, it is truly a study about difference; how it is accepted and how the individuals empower themselves when they are different. The journey for all people of difference is a sojourn from disempowerment to empowerment. However, the population of the study is gay males only, majority and minority inclusive, employed as managers or executives in the business world. Professional groups per se, such as lawyers, doctors, etc., are not included unless they were employed in a corporate setting distinct from their profession. Furthermore, gays in government, social sciences, educational institutions, etc., are not included. The corporations for which the subjects of the study work fit into the traditional definitions of "business," i.e., commercial or mercantile activity engaged in profit. In addition all corporations would be considered as Fortune 500 companies.

This book explores the relationship between the American corporate culture and the gay male frame of reference. In view of the corporate culture's low tolerance for difference, it examines the stages of personal transition from powerlessness to empowerment that gay males move through when confronted with the issue of being gay in the workplace.

The questions addressed are:

- What have gay males experienced as members of straight business organizations?
- Does the model of transition from disempowerment to empowerment, formed from my own experience, hold true for others?
- What enablers permit gay males to continue to move toward empowerment?

This book examines the coping, actualization, and manifestation dynamics of being a gay male and integrating one's self into the workplace.

My discussion of this subject is within a heuristic framework; that is, my personal experience is the lens through which this study was conceived and reported. Such a framework follows the lead of existential philosophers from Socrates to Sartre who postulated that our primary access to reality is through the study of one's own being. My access to being is through opening the doors of my own psyche, my personal study to comprehend and celebrate the experiences that are mine. Furthermore, I use my own experience because there is only one case study I have followed with care and intimacy–my own.

I first used my own experiences as a behavioral model and then proceeded to examine the experience of others who have adapted and/or validated this model of the process for attaining personal and professional actualization and manifestation.

- *Actualization,* herein, is defined as meeting one's total potential, as well as meeting the organizational needs within one's corporate environment.
- *Self-actualization* is existing in act and not merely in potentiality. It is the quality or state of being factual and authentic. Self-actualization, being a state in integrity, brings with it the discovery of full empoweredness.
- *Manifestation* is the state of radiating one's empoweredness and one's integrity.

The movement from actualization to manifestation requires a transformation of an individual's psyche. The key to transformation is acceptance. Out of acceptance comes the celebration of what one is, i.e., his integrity. Celebration causes actualization. Actualization causes manifestation, which is a radiation of what one is. These concepts will be expanded in later chapters.

I share my experiences and build on the experiences of others in this study not as an expert but as an amateur, not because I have found "the answer" but rather because the question has anchored itself in me.

Originally, I proceeded from a paradigm of reference that addressed corporate power and its effect on gays. However, my internal search and external research caused a paradigm shift away from the corporate world–to the individual, his ability and willingness to empower himself, to assert his individuality in his environment.

My actualization showed me that anytime I think the problem is "out there somewhere," the problem is actually with that thought. It is always an inward-outward movement. It is always my piece and their piece. I must be accountable and empowered to work on my piece of the problem whether that be my internalized homophobia or a false belief that attack equals empowerment, before I address the outer, external environment.

The perspective of this study was to test out or understand why and how. It was not to prove; that is, the objective of this effort was to understand why and how gay males in business firms deal with the issues of difference. To do so, the study relied heavily on qualitative as well as quantitative research methods.

The research methods included:

- A heuristic study, that is, a rigorous examination of the writer's personal experiences as a gay executive;
- A review of the scholarly literature in the fields of organizational psychology, empowerment strategies, and gay studies;
- An administration of a Pattern of Reactions Survey to two hundred gay males; and
- In-depth interviews with 40 gay managers/executives.

The heuristic study and the review of the scholarly literature resulted in a six-stage model of transition from disempowerment to empowerment. The surveys and interviews verified the model and identified empowerment enablers.

The data are presented through the process of triangulation. The three angles are:

- The heuristic data;
- The research of the literature; and
- The results of the surveys and interviews.

Throughout this work the male gender, i.e., he, him, and his, will be used because I am only addressing the gay male experience.

The predominant use of the word "gay" in this study is used because "homosexual" is a medical and pathological term with its beginnings in the nineteenth century. The pathological connotations of homosexuality are neither valid nor useful. The word gay predates homosexuality by six centuries and refers to the ontological goodness of the state of being (Boswell, 1980). However, homosexual and heterosexual will be used where deemed appropriate.

This book is intended for gay managers and executives. I hope it provides them with a richer understanding of their psychological and professional sojourn into wholeness. However, anyone interested in people of difference and the study of empowerment should find this work enriching.

The chapters of this book are set up sequentially as in an odyssey.

Chapter 1, "The Need for the Journey," has outlined the purpose and the necessity of this effort.

Chapter 2, "This Is Where We Are," begins with the business community paradigm; the gender of organizations is male and the sexuality of organizations is heterosexual. The movement to accept women as managers and executives has resulted in the famous "glass ceiling." The "glass ceiling"–defined by the U.S. Department of Labor (1991) as the composite of "artificial barriers based on attitudinal or organizational bias that prevent qualified [women] from advancing upward in their organization into [senior] management level positions"–remains nearly as impenetrable as ever. The movement to accept gays and lesbians is virtually nonexistent except for pockets such as Levis, Apple, and Microsoft.

Chapter 2 addresses this dilemma and postulates fundamental concepts that gays must accept as the reality of where we are, if we are to undertake a journey to empowerment. We must know the beginning state before striving for the end state.

Chapter 3, "Drafting the Map," overviews the phenomenological approaches, the strategies to maneuver through the corporate maze, used by gay managers and executives. The coping (surviving), actualization (surviving to striving), and manifestation (striving to thriving) mechanisms are the lines that draft the map.

The map becomes the gay Model of Transition. The model illustrates the "inward-outward" movement necessary to manifestation, the goal of the journey. In the first four stages of the Model, individuals mistakenly begin as if the problem and issues are entirely "out there" phenomena. The first four stages are normal and developmental because they help individuals to realize their contribution to their disempowerment. The fifth stage causes the individual to go inward, causing a transformation of thinking from "because of" to "in relationship to." The sixth stage is the stage of integrity and empowerment.

Distinctions to and definitions of the components of the gay Model of Transition are contained in Chapter 4, "This Is Where We

Must Go.'' As the title indicates, this is a ''desired state.'' The specific emotions and behavior of the individuals as they move through the spiral effect of the Model on their way to empowerment are detailed and described.

Each stage of the transition is described definitionally and motivationally. Empowerment and disempowerment are defined and illustrated. Also, integrity is presented as the core of empowerment and thus the vital ingredient for the movement to Actualization and Manifestation.

Chapter 4, ''This Is Where We Must Go,'' answers the question, ''What enables some to take up the journey, move ahead, and arrive at a state of empowerment?''

Chapter 5, ''On the Road,'' elaborates and expands on Chapter 4, in that the specific action steps by stage of development are delineated. This chapter is crucial, but not wholly understandable if the readers have not immersed themselves in Chapters 1 through 4.

The concrete infrastructures (enablers) that permit and foster the growth and development of empowered gay managers and executives are also discussed.

A step-by-step Proactive Wave Action Plan is presented for consideration and application to the reader's particular work environment.

Chapter 6, ''The Travelog,'' is a summary of the findings from the research conducted to support this book.

Let us now take the journey!

Chapter 2

This Is Where We Are

He has half the deed done, who has made the beginning.

–Horace

The business world, in this century, is not going to mark its place in history for its task side, i.e., its technical accomplishments and communication advances; it is going to be remembered on the human side, as a time in which its leadership stood by, actively supported or passively endorsed the destruction of diversity, especially sexual diversity, unless . . . .

Fulfilling my highest purpose in this century will mean being a communicator, of the way things can be; to search out, tell the story, and persuade the gay and business community to rewrite the future.

It is not the purpose of this book to make a defense of homosexuality, nor is it an attempt to identify cause. Gays are more than sexual beings. A truncated photo of gays has been developed from the preoccupation of literature and researchers with genital activity. Gays' chief gratification in life does not always involve orgasmic sperm release, but rather comes from their self-actualization and manifestation as human beings. They spend their waking hours developing careers, socializing, and exploring personal growth, as do their heterosexual counterparts.

For the purpose of this book, it is sufficient to state two criteria:

1. For whatever reasons, homosexuals do exist as whole, psychologically sound, competent individuals (American Psychiatric Association, 1973 and the American Psychological Association, 1975); and

2. The business community defines and places value judgments on sex and sexual identity.

The former has been extensively documented. The latter is the focus of this chapter.

Freud, as well as common sense, places functionality and soundness on a continuum addressing intimate relationships and work. The point is, if the need and expression of "intimate relationship," whether heterosexual or homosexual, is balanced and whole and therefore does not affect the "work," then let us ignore the issue in the work setting. However, as we will see, it is not simple.

> Beginning with Evelyn Hooker's (1957) study that provided the first empirical evidence that homosexuality per se was not indicative of psychological disturbance, the next two decades witnessed a line of research addressing whether homosexuality per se was indicative of psychological disturbance. As recently reviewed by Gonsiorek (1991), the data overwhelmingly indicate that homosexuality is not indicative of mental illness and theories that continue to purport an illness model of homosexuality represent egregious distortions of scientific information about homosexuality in the service of hatred and bigotry. (Gonsiorek, 1993, p. 244)

Furthermore, employment discrimination and harassment of gays will not be the focus of this chapter or book. Others, namely Hedgeth (1979/80) and Knutson (1979), have well documented this issue. Harassment and discrimination will only be stated in the larger context of the story of this book about empowerment.

Nor will biographical sketches or status issues be addressed. Once again, others such as Gonsiorek (1993), Levine (1989), and Woods and Lucas (1993) have documented these issues.

The business community defines and places value judgments on sex and sexual identity. The business community attributes positive values toward masculinity and heterosexuality and negative values toward femininity and more so toward homosexuality (not that femininity and homosexuality should ever be linked). However, this is very much the corporate paradigm.

From where is this attribution derived? I remember once a colleague suggested that I deal with a difficult client, who happened to be a woman. The colleague said, "Why don't you take this client? Because you're gay, you can probably understand the female psyche better than I." I proceeded to explain to him, rather forcibly, that homosexual meant a preference for men (same) not women. Why would I understand the "female psyche" (his words) more than he? He just did not get it. Be that as it may, the "corporate psyche" purports that femininity and gayness are linked, and that both, as we will see in this chapter, are wrongly equated with professional incompetency, regardless of facts to the contrary.

It can be said that culturally we deal with learned beliefs that condition our behavior. Society has traditionally made sense out of our world in masculine and feminine terms. Men are considered achievers. Women are considered communal. The female role, in the culture-at-large, is predominantly viewed as interpersonal and expressive. The male role is viewed as predominantly achieving and instrumental. These "seen as" roles permeate our society. Being female or male, obviously, is an important aspect of self-identity. Strict adherence to a female or male cultural script, however, may have disastrous results for individuals and organizations.

Alice G. Sargent (Ed., 1977), in the book *Beyond Sex Roles*, elaborates on the point that organizations and individuals who enforce traditional sex-role stereotyping produce a constrictive atmosphere within which creativity and productivity are stifled. The noted psychologist, Sandra Bems (1975), who has been instrumental in fostering the concept of psychological androgyny, stated in a paper presented to the American Psychological Association:

> Extreme femininity, untempered by sufficient concern for one's own needs as an individual, may produce dependency and self-denial, just as extreme masculinity, untempered by a sufficient concern for the needs of others, may produce arrogance and exploitation.

Diagram 2.1 illustrates traditional sex roles which have created a sharp division of labor around sex-linked behaviors (Sargent, 1983, pp. 3-4).

The gender definition of business organizations is male (Wilson, 1979). Everything from organizational planning to performance appraisal systems is geared toward rewarding traditional male attributes. These attitudes are internalized and exhibited both at work and away from work. Alice Sargent (1983), in her book *The Androgynous Manager*, notes:

> Most of the men acknowledged that their expressions of tenderness were usually limited to members of their families, especially to young children. And even displays of tenderness to children, particularly boys, were inhibited by fear of "smothering" them or making them too dependent on their parents. "Doing things is more important than people," said one executive. "In skiing one only needs man and hill; nobody else is necessary."
>
> The men interviewed considered such character traits as strength, self-reliance, and keeping a stiff upper lip as both masculine and conducive to success. One man commented:
>
> "At work one gets accustomed not to express dependence and one does the same at home. As a matter of fact, at work I never think in terms of making good use of available human resources. When I get home, I don't want to talk about any big problem: I just want to rest."
>
> "I group my friends in two ways–those who have made it and don't complain, and those who haven't made it. And only the latter spend time talking to their wives about their problems." (p. 30)

Androgyny, a blending of what are usually regarded as male and female characteristics, values, or attitudes, has as its aim the integration into one's personality of the positive characteristics of the other sex with one's own sex. Androgyny, in the culture-at-large and in the workplace, is little known and therefore little practiced. Movement to an acceptance of gays, as another level, is virtually unheard of and/or practiced. That the workplace is defined as "male" automatically creates a problematic environment for gays. Remember, the corporate paradigm is that gay equals femininity.

Stereotyping also plays a role in the corporate and societal view of homosexuality. The stereotypical heterosexual male is strong,

DIAGRAM 2.1. Traditional Sex Roles

Masculinity	**Femininity**
•Compliance producing	•Alliance producing
•Directive	•Collaborative
•Task oriented	•Climate oriented
•Toughness	•Tenderness
•Autonomy	•Connectedness
•Think then do	•Feel then do
• Instrumental or problem solving	•Concern for others' welfare and group cohesiveness
•"Agent orientation"–a concern for oneself as an individual	•"Communal orientation"– a concern for one's relationship to others
•Competition and responsiveness to crisis–responding to new ideas and having an individual impact	•Collaboration and teamwork– responding with personal trust, openness, and democratic leadership
•Strength and self-reliance equal success	• Interdependence and expressed emotions equal success

independent, and competent. The stereotypical homosexual male, assumed to have feminine characteristics, is seen as weak, dependent, and incompetent.

Richard Zoglin (1979), in *What It's Like to Be Gay in a Pin-Striped World*, elaborates on the myth of the heterosexual male as being strong and the homosexual male as being weak by illustrating how difficult and almost impossible it is for the male homosexual to break down this mythology and receive deserved promotions. Peter Fisher (1978) in *The Gay Mystique* points out the false link made between homosexuality and femininity:

Some people are willing to concede that homosexuals have as much right to work as anyone else, but hasten to add that there are some types of employment for which they are unsuited.

All homosexuals are effeminate–they are not fit for men's work. (p. 154)

In addition, society's perception of the homosexual is fraught with sexual overtones. Compare the definition of terms in *Webster's New Collegiate Dictionary*:

heterosexual (adj.)	1. of, relating to, or marked by heterosexuality.
	2. of or relating to different sexes.
homosexual (adj.)	of, relating to, or exhibiting sexual desire toward a member of one's own sex.
heterosexual (n.)	a heterosexual individual.
homosexual (n.)	one who is inclined toward or practices homosexuality.
heterosexuality (n.)	the manifestation of sexual desire for one or more members of the opposite sex.
homosexuality (n.)	1. the manifestation of sexual desire for one's own sex.
	2. erotic activity with a member of one's own sex.

The innuendo is implicit in the definitions. A heterosexual is simply a "heterosexual *individual*," whereas a homosexual is "one who is inclined toward or practices homosexuality." One exists in a "state of being"; the other is defined by his sexual behavior. Further, while both definitions state "manifestation of sexual desire" for the opposite or same sex, only the definition for homosexuality is given a second entry: erotic activity. The value-laden term "erotic activity" underlines society's preoccupation with the homosexual's orientation which is apparently lacking in its reaction to a heterosexual. In short, the homosexual is easily seen in the bedroom, but not in the board room!

It would seem, then, that there are three concepts at work in corporations with which gays must deal–that of traditional sex roles and the division of labor, stereotyping, and preoccupation with sexual orientation at the expense of the whole individual.

In 1985 the National Association of Business Councils, an association of gay and lesbian businesspersons, conducted a study of major American corporations in 23 cities across the country in order to:

1. determine existing corporate policies and practices with reference to lesbian and gay employees; and
2. sensitize the corporations to and inform them of the special needs of lesbian and gay employees.

Only one of the 23 cities, San Francisco, had corporate policies or procedures to prohibit discrimination based on sexual preference in terms of competence in the performance of employees. The notable absence of such policies indicates a tremendous need to sensitize corporations to this issue.

Organizationally, the stereotyping of each sex and sexual preference relative to competence has disastrous results in terms of heavy employee turnover and financial losses. However, it exists to the point that it is the "unspoken way." Stereotyping is caused by prejudice and traditional myths that keep gays stuck. The biggest prejudicial obstacle for gays is also the most intangible. My research shows that straight men, at the top, feel uncomfortable with gay males beside them. Straight men are much more comfortable dealing with other heterosexual males. Traditional, organizational myths are subtle and unconscious. When confronted by blatant, prevailing prejudice, the straight males interviewed resorted to the argument of "It was not our intent." No one is questioning intent. Many, however, are pointing to the *outcome* of straight prejudiced behavior, which is damaging.

Both intention and outcome must be a part of any discussion regarding the management of diversity. However, what the straight male intended is as important as what the gay experienced. Too often, the straight organizational male gets stuck on intent because it is more comfortable for majority groups to focus on personal intent as the shield of protection for the negative, disastrous results of their behavior and the institutionalized behavior which is the measurable observable outcome: gay males rarely get promoted above middle-level management, if they are known to be gay. Where are the gay presidents, vice presidents, or even chairpersons of the board? Can the reader name them as easily as one can name their heterosexual counterparts? I doubt it. Some, like Forbes, have to be "outed" or die before the general public knows. If they are there, they are living in marriages of convenience or, sadly, truly marriages of deception. In my consulting work and during the research for this book I found them. Only one president, however, would be in the Actualization and Manifestations stage of our model. However, the others in the Actualization and Manifestation stage will soon step into those positions. Maybe! This is the way it is.

Blatantly false organizational stereotyping equates with instability. One straight executive interviewed stated: "Just see how they (gays) behave openly different when out of the supervision of the corporation!" If one equates homosexuality with instability, etc., then one assumes that gay males will have unstable work records. In a 1973 study (Saghir and Robins, 1973), homosexual men were found to have held more full-time jobs, and to have put in more hours, but to have been fired more often than heterosexual men.

A 1978 job stability study (Bell and Weinberg, 1978) showed that almost half of the homosexual males in a same sample size of 5,000, had not changed jobs at all in the last five years. Homosexual and heterosexual men did not differ with regard to how many voluntary job changes occurred within five years. However, as Saghir and Robins found, homosexual men were fired more often for nonmeasurable reasons.

However, heterosexual men were promoted at three times the rate of their equally competent, and often harder-working, homosexual counterparts. This is the way it is.

The Greater Washington Business and Professional Council found that, frustrated by the strain of fighting what seemed to be unassailable barriers, hundreds of the brightest gay males have left corporations, and established successful businesses, ranging from manufacturing endeavors to consulting firms. The gay president of a successful five million dollar consulting firm, interviewed during my study, stated, "The only way to reach your goals is by jumping off the corporate ladder and pursuing entrepreneurial endeavors." This is the way it is.

Up to a certain point brains and competence count for something in the corporate world. But fitting in becomes more important. It is at this point that the subtle, invisible barriers go up. Male bonding takes place on the golf course with other heterosexual males. Their gay counterparts are neither invited nor wanted.

All this is to say that most American corporations have, unconsciously for the most part, developed a corporate climate within which the corporation defines itself as male and heterosexual (Wilson, 1979). Consider Diagram 2.2, which illustrates the corporate definition of competency.

The diagram is the "appropriate" model. The appropriate model is the myth of commonly accepted assumptions that are not ques-

DIAGRAM 2.2. Corporate Definition of Competency

RACE:	White	
SEX:	Male	
PHYSICAL APPEARANCE:	Attractive (Tall and Thin)	ORGANIZATIONAL DESIRABLES
RELIGION:	Protestant	(Competency as Viewed by the Organizations)
FINANCIAL BACKGROUND:	Affluent	
FAMILY STATUS:	Married/Children	
SEXUAL PREFERENCE:	Heterosexual	

tioned or investigated by the majority of those working within corporate America. The collective identity, the appropriate model, of the straight male majority occurs because the group members do not see the accumulated impact of their individual behavior on the gay male. A gay will experience one straight male telling an obnoxious AIDS joke, another initiating a conversation in a ridiculing homophobic manner, another making overt homosexually biased slurs–all in the same day. The gay male experiences the accumulated impact. If the gay reacts publicly, the heterosexual male cannot or will not understand the magnitude of the problem and so employs the appropriate, white, male, tall and thin, Protestant, affluent, married with children, heterosexual model and says, "We don't act like this, therefore you're wrong!"

Given the "appropriateness" of the model, the more divergence from the model, the less tolerance exhibited by the organization as a whole. One who conforms to the model is "appropriate" for the corporate environment.

> The way our privates behave is a matter of public policy. Uncle Sam is watching you and so is General Motors. The man who comes home exhausted because he has been taught to believe without question that his male identity is based on nine-to-five loyalty and the giving of his best energies to the corporation has made a decision about his sexuality. He sacrifices his corpus to the corporation. His chosen method of expanding energy and structuring time disallows afternoon dalliance with his wife or lover. (Keen, 1983, p. 101)

Change one "box" in the model and the individual is seen as less competent and usually has to "try harder" in order to overcome this organizational "handicap." For instance, if we hypothetically change the Family Status box from married to single, we are left with a white male, single, etc. Now let us say the organization holds a cocktail party and invites our single white male. Knowing the cultural script so well, he will probably bring to the party an attractive white female. The scenario at the party will probably be that all the married white males will corner the attractive white female. Most of the married females will feel intimidated and choose to avoid our hypothetical couple.

Meanwhile, who is being left out of the communication flow and relationship-building dynamic? Our single white male! He is going to have to "try harder" to get into the relationship-building activities that are so vital in large corporations. Meanwhile, the corporate cultural script is being written deeper. This is the way it is.

Now let's change all the boxes to some "undesirable" categories. (See Diagram 2.3.) Visualize the intensity of organizational intolerance for this individual. Unlike our single white male, our single African-American lesbian was probably "quietly" not invited to the cocktail party. Visualize her tremendous sense of powerlessness in her corporate world.

Given this, some have asked me, "Why didn't you focus your work on African-American lesbian managers and executives?" The answer is quite simple. "I'm not female, African-American, etc." A lesbian's experience in the workplace is inevitably different from a gay's, if only from the perspective that the gay may ultimately have the "male privilege" to fall back on.

There is no doubt that the above African-American lesbian must experience multiple oppression. Therefore, I encourage and support an African-American lesbian in the conduct of such a study.

Gayle Rubin forcibly points out this phenomenon by describing a

DIAGRAM 2.3. Corporate Definition of Incompetency

RACE:	African-American	
SEX:	Female	
PHYSICAL APPEARANCE:	Unattractive (short and overweight)	ORGANIZATIONAL UNDESIRABLES
RELIGION:	Islamic	(Incompetency as Viewed by the Organizations)
FINANCIAL BACKGROUND:	Unprosperous	
FAMILY STATUS:	Single/Childless	
SEXUAL PREFERENCE:	Homosexual	

pyramid made up of levels to the corporate system of a sexual caste system:

> Modern Western societies appraise sex acts according to a hierarchical system of sexual value. Marital, reproductive heterosexuals are alone at the top of the erotic pyramid. Clamoring below are unmarried monogamous heterosexuals in couples, followed by most other heterosexuals. Solitary sex floats ambiguously. . . . Stable, long-term lesbian and gay male couples are verging on respectability, but bar dykes and promiscuous gay men are hovering just above the groups at the very bottom of the pyramid. (Rubin, 1984, p. 279)

Given the construct that organizations have been traditionally defined in masculine and feminine attributes; given that this construct moves to another frame of heterosexual and homosexual attributes; and given that organizational androgynous models are by and large unheard of and unpracticed, it was the experience of the subjects of this study that the above assumptions transferred into organizational power dynamics of conversion and domination. Organizations, indeed, have a theology of conversion and dominance that is founded on a belief of heterosocial superiority and elitism. Egalitarianism is generally an unknown and unpracticed virtue.

"Conversion" occurs when someone is transformed by external forces from one purpose to another. "Dominance" is the state of being forcibly kept in a particular condition. Conversion arises as a consequence of unconscious organizational pressures for sameness. This dynamic requires that gays look, think, and act like their heterosexual counterparts. This is obviously easier for the white gay male than the gay male of color. If the conversion strategy is applied, it makes one "dance to the same drummer."

I personally experienced the conversion and dominance dynamic when I was a senior analyst at a large biochemical research firm. My executive vice president, when informed that I was gay, immediately went into a conversion stance. His strategies were: logic and reason; persuasion by refusing business rewards, that is, new projects were given to less-experienced colleagues; and recognition for any aggressive male stereotypic behaviors. In an abrasive, confrontational meeting, he pointed out the "error of my ways" and elaborated on the negative consequences to my position and career if I continued to be a "dissident." He concluded the meeting with a reminder that the firm could provide psychiatric help. His point was clear: come over to the "straight" side and be saved!

At this point, I was "partially" in the closet and therefore acquiesced. I noticed that I would literally receive pats on the back for talking with peers about what my "girlfriend" and I did over the weekend.

When I became frustrated with my own lack of integrity and discontinued the behaviors, my boss adopted the dominance stance. His strategies were: monitoring "unacceptable" behaviors, and evaluating activities and tasks on the basis of "appropriateness" by sexual scripts. One of his most violent outbursts occurred when he walked into the office coffee lounge and "caught" me cleaning the coffee counter and shouted, "For Christsakes, will you stop acting like somebody's wife!" I was astounded by his outburst. He had cleaned the counter many times. I concluded that he saw homosexuality as femininity and saw femininity where femininity did not exist.

An acrimonious atmosphere ensued. The results of which were: I moved away and disengaged from business socialization; a keen sense of powerlessness engulfed me; my analytical focus, vital to a senior analyst, diminished; and overall productivity plunged. Thus, my behavior illustrated to my boss that his assumptions about gays as being weak and incompetent were proven.

One hundred percent (40) of the participants interviewed described similar experiences.

Diagram 2.4 illustrates the Conversion and Dominance Dynamic. The diagram is true only when one is in the Reactive stage, which will be addressed in Chapter 3.

The Conversion and Dominance Dynamic creates probabilistic causality. The relationship is one of producer-product, a cause-and-effect relationship, resulting from a mechanistic approach rather than a teleological approach. The Greek word "teleological" means "purposeful" rather than deterministic causality. To illustrate, it is true that one cannot have an oak without an acorn. An acorn is clearly necessary to an oak, but it is not sufficient. If one takes an acorn and puts it in a dark closet, one will not get an oak tree. One

DIAGRAM 2.4. The Conversion and Dominance Dynamic

1. Homosexuality of the individual becomes known.
   Attempts are made by the establishment to *convert* through:

   logic and reason
   persuasion through denial of rewards
   reward for not being like one's own kind

2. Individual acquiesces and/or returns to the closet, if not:
   Attempts are made by the establishment to *dominate* through:

   monitoring unacceptable behaviors
   evaluating on the basis of "appropriateness" by sex and cultural scripts

3. An acrimonious environment occurs.

4. Resulting in the individual's:

   moving away and disengaging
   personal powerlessness
   loss of productivity

5. Resulting in affirmations by the organization (self-fulfilling prophecy) that the
   prototype is correct, based on the loss of productivity.

will not get an oak if one puts an acorn on top of a rock or in sand with no water–all sorts of other things, from a teleological point of view, are necessary. One only gets an oak tree by preserving its integrity and supporting its individual growth needs.

The model presented in Chapter 3 illustrates stages of empowerment rather than the dynamics of disempowerment illustrated above. It is "teleological."

Kanter and Stein (1980) describe a concept similar to my Conversion and Dominance Dynamic through descriptors X and O. X is the majority. O is the minority.

Becoming a superstar O.
This is how a few very talented O's have always been able to succeed among the X's. (p. 56)

Some O's make a second choice: They try to look like an X, to blend into the crowd and become less visible by wearing X clothing, using X mannerisms and X language, or acting like an X. (p. 62)

So some O's make a third choice: They avoid the competition altogether and step out of the spotlight, by hiding behind an X or taking a job performing under constant pressure. The O can be just an assistant–the person who writes the report but doesn't deliver it in public. Some O's have always settled for helping someone else advance; for vicarious achievement through pushing someone else's career. You know what they say: "Behind every great X is an O." (p. 64)

This last choice, dropping out, has led to a popular conclusion: "O's fear success." (p. 66)

The O is forced to play a particular part because of the nature of the situation it is in–in this case, being one of very few of its kind among many of another kind. The O's choices are limited: it is forced to act in predictable ways. (p. 204)

Organizations usually accept heterosexual masculine qualities as appropriate organizational behavior (X) and suppress or "convert" the gay qualities (O). Under these circumstances, conflict is extremely difficult, if not impossible, to resolve. Furthermore, organizations perceive, understand, accept, and tolerate masculine behavior only from men, and feminine behavior only from women. Androgynous behavior, in most cases, is neither perceived, understood, accepted, nor tolerated. This Conversion and Dominance Dynamic, where it exists, has created a keen sense of powerlessness for women and men in the workplace, but especially for gays and lesbians.

Domination/Conversion exacerbates the basic organizational problem of reaching resolution by either approving or challenging an individual's ideas, techniques, and behaviors as they fit the concept of "appropriateness."

On an interpersonal level, it challenges the right of the gay male to be who he is, which is a homosexual. It requires him to deny his spirit. This is the way it is!

And now AIDS, a devastating disease in and of itself, is added to the list of reasons to discriminate against gays in the workplace.

On the societal level, The Center for Disease Control conservatively estimates that presently (1994), 1.5 million Americans are HIV positive. Every county in the United States has at least one AIDS case.

To the society-at-large, AIDS is new and frightening. The impact of the AIDS epidemic is significant for business. Ninety percent of those with AIDS are between 25 and 49 years old, the workforce age.

The following article appeared in the October 13, 1988 edition of *USA Today*.

"Many Would Discriminate Over AIDS"

One out of 4 people wouldn't want AIDS sufferers in their workplaces, neighborhoods and schools, a review of opinion polls shows.

And most believe widespread AIDS testing would lead to discrimination against those testing positive, researchers report in today's *New England Journal of Medicine*.

"The average man on the street knows that if you get tested for AIDS and get a positive result, you can lose your job and your home," says Robert J. Blendon of the Harvard School of Public Health, Boston, who reviewed 53 polls conducted over the past five years.

Blendon says the polls also reveal a great deal of hostility:

–More than 1 in 4 favors a tattoo for infected people.

–1 in 5 believes AIDS patients are getting their due for improper behavior.

– 1 in 2 says AIDS patients don't merit compassion.

Given these attitudes, new anti-discrimination laws may be the only way to protect infected people from unfair treatment, Blendon says.

Kim Painter, USA Today

In 1986 and again in 1988, political extremist Lyndon LaRouche placed propositions on the California ballot that if passed would have quarantined people with AIDS, and those showing positive to the test could be fired. It took nearly half a million signatures to qualify the measure for the ballot. Thus, the numbers testify to the popularity of discrimination, even in such an otherwise liberal state.

Some would say that was the 1970s and 1980s, and that in the 1990s society and business have attitudinally progressed. Not so. Go, seek out, and listen to anyone who is HIV positive or who has AIDS and hear their stories. Pick up a local gay publication and read the horror stories about discrimination and dismissal. One has only to watch the movie *Philadelphia* to get the point . . . "Well . . . my God, he brought AIDS into our office and to our families."

Nancy Roth and Judith Carman's extensive research regarding HIV and the workplace stated:

> This research suggests that knowledge and attitudes about HIV are often widely divergent. Although workers "know" that the risk of HIV transmission in their workplaces is negligible, they still would prefer that their workplaces not hire HIV positive workers and prefer not to interact with such coworkers. (Roth and Carman, 1993, p. 177)

Their surveys yielded the following:

> Our findings concerning attitudes and fears about HIV/AIDS were consistent with the literature. Thirty-five percent of our respondents would not be willing to eat in a restaurant where they know the chef has HIV, 17% would not want to send their children to school with a child who has HIV, and 58% do not believe that scientists know all there is to know about how HIV is transmitted. (Roth and Carman, 1993, p. 181)

And the antigay bias in the AIDS epidemic is demonstrated by another study.

> Three hundred undergraduate students were asked about their attitudes toward different fictionalized characters described in short vignettes. Their character differed only on their specific illnesses (AIDS versus leukemia) and their sexual orientation (gay versus heterosexual). Homosexual patients

were considered more responsible for, and more deserving of, their illnesses, more deserving of employment loss, and less deserving of sympathy and even medical care. (St. Lawrence et al., 1990)

AIDS is new and frightening to American corporations. The subject is so loaded with bias, contention, and misinformation that it adds another level of conscious and unconscious discrimination.

AIDS molds behavior in many ways. In the worst, usually hushed-up incidents, employees afraid of AIDS-carrying co-workers have walked off the job. More common are dances of avoidance–workers refusing to share tools or even sit in the cafeteria with a stricken coworker. And then there is a very different reaction–grief at the loss of a friend and colleague. In a society where, for many, the workplace isn't merely the source of a paycheck but also a source of community, where fellow workers are also friends, there is simply no way for business to wall out AIDS. (Krip, 1989, p.142)

All this is to say that little is being done about AIDS discrimination in corporations. Barely one business in ten has a written AIDS policy (Krip, 1989). However, Pacific Bell, a traditionally conservative organization, had responded with what David Krip has called "uncommon decency." Levi Strauss, another leader, sponsored the first-ever conference on "AIDS in the Workplace," on March 29, 1986. Some 200 managers from 100 companies attended. However, across the nation most companies persist in punishing workers with AIDS and have used AIDS as another tool to discriminate against gays in the workplace. This is the way it is.

Frequently through this chapter I have stated: "This is the way it is." The point is that the business community paradigm is: the gender of organizations is male and the sexuality of organizations is heterosexual. The result is that being gay is seen as weak and incompetent. Therefore, discrimination, covert or overt, is the way it is.

This chapter had been descriptive. Chapter 3, "Drafting the Map," is prescriptive. It overviews the phenomenological approaches of gay managers and executives. The gay Model of Transition in Corporations is presented and described.

Chapter 3

Drafting the Map

What we call the beginning
is often the end
And to make an end
is to make a beginning
The end
is where we start from.

–T.S. Eliot

The road map of reality is difficult indeed. Our view of ourselves and our reality is like a map with which we negotiate the terrain of our existence. If the map is accurate, up-to-date, illustrative, and true, we generally know where we are. Therefore, if we decide we want to go elsewhere, we will know how to get there. If the map is false, inaccurate, based upon conjecture and mythology, we will get lost or at least go around in circles.

Although the above may seem obvious, it is also something that most people, to a greater or lesser degree, choose to ignore. We ignore it because it demands a dedication to reality and introspection. Such dedication is hard! Our road map of reality is difficult indeed.

We must close our eyes and invoke a new manner of seeing . . . a wakefulness that is the birthright of us all, though few put it to use. (Plotinus, 1964, p. 42)

The coping, actualization, and manifestation mechanisms of gays at work in the corporate environment is the map that will be examined in this chapter. The stages of transition from disempowerment to empowerment are presented and discussed.

The psychological dynamics of gays at work in the corporate environment are as varied as gay individuals themselves. However, a common phenomenological approach seems to be emerging.

It can easily be said that reality is truth and that which is false is unreal, or "believing is seeing." However, the more accurately we see the reality of the world, that of problems and pain with actualization and manifestation, the more we are equipped to design our road maps, those tools for coping, dealing, managing, and transcending.

The first of the "Four Noble Truths" which Buddha taught was "Life is Suffering." Peck takes a softer interpretation of the Buddhist principle by saying, "Life is Difficult."

> Life is Difficult. This is a great truth, one of the greatest truths. It is a great truth because once we truly see this truth, we transcend it. Once we truly know that life is difficult–once we truly understand and accept it–then life is no longer difficult. Because once it is accepted, the fact that life is difficult no longer matters. (Peck, 1987, p. 15)

When I first heard of the Noble Truths, I strongly resented and resisted them; I thought they were self-indulgent and pessimistic. But as Stephen Levine (1979) states:

> But seeing the scope of my wanting showed me how deeply and subtly dissatisfaction created my personal world, and that seeing freed me from much grasping . . . . (p. 14)

It is my purpose to focus on the positive rather than the negative by saying "Life is Suffering." One of the principles of psychology and a tenet in many world religions is: first, spending one's time and energy intellectually musing, "Why is it so?" or second, trying to make pain (existential angst) go away, is more psychologically and spiritually painful and less harmonious than accepting "Life is Suffering." Rising above the pain, designing a psychological map that says, "In spite of . . . " moves one away from a "victimized," reactive stand to a proactive and/or coactive empowered stand.

Existential psychology can best be summarized by the central idea of Heidegger's philosophy of ontology: that man is a "being-in-the-world." Thus one must focus on the meaning that he gives to his existence and to his mode of being in the world that he specifically has chosen.

Maladaptive behavior, from the existential psychologist's point of view, distinguishes between two types of suffering–existential and neurotic.

Existential suffering is the legitimate pain of being, elicited by existential issues such as:

- The threat of non-being;
- The necessity to make choices in the face of uncertainty; and
- The knowledge that one can never know, in this life, what it "feels" like to be someone else.

This existential angst is not pathological or maladaptive, but instead is an inevitable consequence of the human condition.

Neurotic suffering is not the legitimate pain of being. It is elicited by anxiety. Anxiety has no foundation, it is illusionary, even though it may seem real at the time to the person. Neurotic suffering based on illusionary anxiety results when a person does not accept the reality of existential suffering. The individual usually holds an attitude that, "It shouldn't be this way!" Neurotic suffering thus occurs when one:

- First, does not accept existential suffering, and
- Second, attempts to make the pain of the human condition, existential pain, go away.

It is an attempt to evade the legitimate existential angst necessary for psychological and spiritual growth. The neurotic sufferer has stopped being accountable, has stopped taking responsibility for his own life and his choices, which eventually leads to the dysfunctional victim status of being hopeless and helpless. Although neurotic suffering can take many forms, it most commonly involves a decrease in one's sense of self-as-instrumental (proactive/coactive) and a corresponding increase in one's sense of self-as-object (victim/reactive) (Keen, 1970).

Scott Peck, in his most recent publication, *Further Along the Road Less Traveled* (1994), calls existential suffering "constructive suffering," and neurotic suffering "unconstructive suffering." Unconstructive suffering is something one should make every effort not to experience. Constructive suffering needs to be worked through in order to achieve psychological and spiritual growth. It is an inward-to-outward development, which I will elaborate on at a later point in this book. Put dogmatically, one must do the inner work of dealing with existential angst before one can do the outer work of being an effective gay manager or executive.

Peck offers a simple but effective question: "Is this pain enhancing my existence or limiting it?" (Peck, 1994, p. 22). Is the angst existential suffering or is it neurotic? The point is well made. Existential suffering is enhancing and appropriate. Go with it!

Authentic existence requires the mode of being-in-the-world, which I am calling the Coactive Wave of the Actualization and Manifestation Phase of the Gay Model of Transition detailed in this chapter. Authentic existence, integrity, is a state of empowerment which requires one to do one's inner work and move from disempowerment to empowerment.

Now, back to our map. We are not born with the definition of reality on our road map; we have to define, design, and implement, all of which are painful. Once again, as with road mapping, all too often we choose to avoid pain. As so precisely stated by Carl Jung, "Neurosis is always a substitute for legitimate suffering" (Levine, 1979, p. 14). By "legitimate suffering," I mean disciplining one's self to see beyond the pain; the means by which we embrace the pain of problems in such a way is to work them through, solve them successfully, learning and growing in the process.

We cannot solve life's problems except by solving them. This statement may seem ideologically tautological or self-evident, yet it is seemingly beyond the comprehension of much of the human race. This is because we must accept responsibility for a problem by saying "It is not my problem." We cannot solve a problem by hoping that someone else will solve it for us. I can solve a problem only when I say, "This is my problem and it's up to me to solve it." But many, so many, seek to avoid the pain of their problems by saying to themselves: "This problem was caused me by other people, or by social circumstances beyond my control, and therefore it is up to other people of society to solve this problem for me. It is not really my personal problem." (Peck, 1978, pp. 32-33)

If we choose to live by avoiding pain, saying "This is not my problem," we choose, in the language of the gay culture, "to suffer the tyranny of the closet." If we choose "coming out," it is almost as if a delicate statuette in a fragile Fabergé egg stepped out of its protective shell into reality. However, in the process of "coming out," we have defined our reality as good and wholesome. We design our road maps accordingly.

As the years tick by, more gays are out of the closet in celebration of who they are. This new status calls for new and different strategies for dealing and managing. The old coping strategies are gone forever when the closet door closes behind us.

In the move toward Actualization and Manifestation rather than coping strategies, I cannot help but be reminded of *Alice in Wonderland*.

Alice thought she had never seen such a curious croquet-ground in her life: it was all ridges and furrows; the croquet balls were live hedgehogs, and the mallets live flamingos, and the soldiers had to double themselves up and stand on their hands and feet, to make the arches.

The chief difficulty Alice found at first was in managing her flamingo: she succeeded in getting its body tucked away, comfortably enough, under her arm with its legs hanging, but generally, just as she had got its neck nicely straightened out, and was going to give the hedgehog a blow with its head it would twist itself round and look up at her face, with such a puzzled expression that she could not help bursting out laughing; and when she had got its head down, and was going to begin again, it was very provoking to find that the hedgehog had unrolled itself, and was in the act of crawling away; besides all this, there was generally a ridge or furrow in the way wherever she wanted to send the hedgehog to, and, as the doubled-up soldiers were always getting up and walking off to other parts of the ground, Alice soon came to the conclusion that it was a very difficult game indeed. (Carroll, 1990)

Those of us who decide to try our hands at actualization and manifestation have, like Alice, chosen a very difficult game indeed. The ringing words, "Off with their heads," echo in the back of our minds as we attempt to be who we are and offer that specialness to our corporation.

Organizations are alive, wiggling and twisting like Alice's flamingo. When you think you have identified a problem, it may well "get up and walk away" before you can solve it. "Ridges" and "furrows" are to be found everywhere to block the path of what seems to be rational progress. And when the flamingo looks you straight in the eye and says, "You, too, are part of the problem," it is good to be able to laugh and recognize the humor in the situation, for we *are* part of the problem (Ingalls, 1976, p. 201).

As stated, the psychological dynamics of gays at work in the corporate environment are as varied as gay individuals themselves. However, a common phenomenological approach seems to be emerging. That common phenomenological approach is self-actualization and outward manifestation. This takes place by following the stages of transition from disempowerment to empowerment.

The word "stages" implies the psychological metaphor that life is a journey. If there are stages, there are maps. If there are maps, there are choices of journeys to be taken. A journey requires an end-state, a point, a vision of somewhere else, a purpose, a destination toward which the process of taking steps is moving.

The Latin word for a journey of endeavor is *conatus*, which means striving toward something. The steps, the movement, have a "point-cause." They have a *Logos* (a worshipped reason). This conatus (striving) is not a contingent aspect of a thing, nor is it an element in its being along with other elements; it is its *essentia actualis*. The conatus makes one who one is; so that if the conatus disappears, the self disappears. Striving toward self-affirmation and manifestation makes one what one is. Spinoza calls this striving "the essence of being" and also its power; and he says of the mind: the mind that affirms (*affirmat sive povit*) creates its own power of action (*ipsius agendi potemtiam*) (Durant, 1961).

There is a journey that gays take as they progress from disempowerment to empowerment. As earlier stated, not all choose to take it. In suggesting the analogy of a journey, I wish us to view the traveling as a circular movement, a spiral upward. It is not a linear movement which calls for a before and after. It is a spiral upward in the sense that it is symphonic progression; each movement is built upon a previous movement. It is infinite.

The word "transition" implies an evolutionary process between and linkage to the next stage.

> What is a transition?
> A transition is a discontinuity in a person's life space. Sometimes the discontinuity is defined by social consensus as to what constitutes a discontinuity within the culture. Van Gennep (1960) emphasizes the importance of publicly recognized rites and rituals which demarcate the transition. He talks of a "status passage" from separation through the transition to the incorporation of a new role (Adams, Hays, and Hapson, 1976, p. 5)

A transition calls for a movement from a present state to an "altered" future state. During a transition, modification of consciousness occurs, followed by behavior anchors (Wilhelm-Buckley and Perkins, 1984). Beckhard and Harris (1977) define transition as the period of time and state of affairs that exist between an identification of need and the achievement of a desired future state (p. 56).

We are back to our metaphor of a spiral within the transformation process, because the desired state is not always within sight and therefore the progress is not linear.

It is also important to make a distinction between change and transition. Change is a process of altering, modifying, and refashioning, where to transit is an act of metamorphosis. William Bridges (1986) aptly makes the distinction between change and transition:

> Since change and transition are often used interchangeably, let me clarify the difference between them. Change happens when something starts or stops, or when something that used to happen in one way starts happening in another. It happens at a particular time, or in several stages at different times.

> Transition, on the other hand, is a three-part psychological process that extends over a long period of time and cannot be planned or managed by the same rational formula that work with change. (p. 25)

Individuals in transition must undergo the three-part psychological processes addressed by Bridges (1986) as follows:

1. They have to let go of the old situation and (what is more difficult) of the old identity that went with it.
2. They have to go through the "neutral zone" between their old reality and a new reality that may still be very unclear.
3. They have to make a new beginning, a beginning that is much more than the relatively simple "new start" required in change.

The statement "new beginning" perhaps does not do justice to the struggle as these individuals move to the next wrenching transition point and begin again to the next phase. "Reborn" is perhaps the most appropriate word. What I address in this chapter is not change or the process of adjustment; it is the process of choosing transformation. It is the process of metamorphosis to the transformation from the larva state to the butterfly.

Permit me to tell an ancient but well-known story that I believe illustrates what I am addressing. Moses understood well, in his century, the transitional phases described in this century by Bridges. A segmented, linear view of the journey to the Promised Land is that the shortest distance between two points is a straight line. Not so by our spiral, organic view. Moses was not dumb! He knew that to help his people deal with change and transition they must wander in the desert. The "wandering" was the time period within which some of his people could die out, i.e., those who chose not to deal with the change or could not accept the pain of transition. Wandering causes wondering. It provided the time frame needed for building readiness and willingness, the support necessary for a mental and a capacity shift from a self-perception of slaves to a self-perception of "chosen people." Only a mental shift, i.e., accepting the change as necessary and the willingness to see beyond the pain of transition, can allow creative visualization: seeing one's self before arriving, not as a disempowered slave or displaced wanderer, but rather as a "chosen (empowered) person," proactively and coactively functioning in a Promised Land.

In this book I provide a model of transition which other gay males and I have experienced in corporate America. In making a transformational change from disempowerment to empowerment, each stage and especially each transition point offers a unique potential for personal insight, growth, transformation and, above all, manifestation to others who may be embarking on such an odyssey. In this transitional journey, the stages are:

1. Denial and Minimization
2. Retreat and Isolation
3. Anger and Conflict
4. Depression and Victimization
5. Internalization and Transformation, and
6. Actualization and Manifestation.

This odyssey can be very confusing and filled with turmoil and pain. As addressed earlier, "legitimate suffering" is to discipline one's self to see beyond the pain to the fruits of the devoted pilgrimage.

> There is nothing more difficult to take in hand, more perilous to conduct, than to take the lead in the introduction of a new order of things, because the innovation has for enemies all those who have done well under the old condition and lukewarm defenders in those who may do well under the new. (Niccolo Machiavelli, 1981, p. 51)

For an individual to arrive at manifestation, the process involves movement from Denial-Minimization to Actualization-Manifestation. Diagram 3.1 illustrates the spiral movement.

In development/transitional literature, the path from A to B is often illustrated as a spiral ascent. It may have stages, phases, steps, etc., but the purpose is an apparent fixed-desire state. Although it may seem like a labyrinth, with many side journeys with multichoice pathways, the TAO (the way) is direct although a spiral ascent. In this case, it is indeed an odyssey. Odysseus' purpose and end-state is clear—empowerment—but the sojourn is much larger and

DIAGRAM 3.1. Spiral Movement of Stages

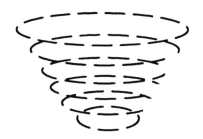

VI. Actualization and
     Manifestation

V.   Internalization and
     Transformation

IV. Depression and
     Victimization

III. Anger and Conflict

II. Retreat and Isolation

I.   Denial and Minimization

more twisted than he imagines at the beginning point. Odysseus was called "a man of many turns." A gay manager or executive must be Odysseus. The shortest distance between point a, disempowerment, to point b, empowerment, is not a straight line; it is a spiral ascent.

It is often difficult to address the complexity of the factors involved in such transitions. However, for the purpose of this study, I have found it illustrative to delineate and characterize three major waves of transition:

- Reactive: self as a result of the situation;
- Proactive: self as a part of the situation;
- Coactive: self as instrumental in the situation.

Diagram 3.2 illustrates the connection between the stages of transition and waves of transition. Reactive (self as a result of the situation) entails reacting to a situation as if it were something totally outside one's sphere of influence. This wave contains the first four stages of transition. The primary results of this wave are:

- Self-orientation;
- Disempowerment;
- Overt displays of anger, hurt, and victimization.

DIAGRAM 3.2. Waves of Transition

STAGE	WAVE
I. Denial and Minimization	REACTIVE– Self as a result of the situation
II. Retreat and Isolation	
III. Anger and Conflict	
IV. Depression and Victimization	
V. Internalization and Transformation	PROACTIVE– Self as a part of the situation
VI. Actualization and Manifestation	COACTIVE– Self as instrumental in the situation

It is a paradigm that is false. The Reactive Wave is rooted in the belief that the entire problem is "out there somewhere," wholly outside the individual. We will see that individuals in the Proactive Wave realize their piece of the program, that is, victims can only exist if they are willing to have persecutors. Individuals in the Coactive Wave achieve totally satisfying and harmonious strategies that result in the highest good for all concerned.

Although the Reactive Wave is a starting point, and everyone must experience it, sadly, the research behind this book shows that of the 200 gay managers and executives surveyed, 81 percent (162) believe that the Reactive Wave is the "right way."

Self-orientation and disempowerment are motivated by the need for survival, security, and acceptance. Deficiency motivation is the foundation for the overt displays of anger, hurt, and victimization. According to the noted sociologist Abraham Maslow (1965), *deficiency motivation* is the absence of satisfaction relative to ungratified wishes, in this case, safety, security, and acceptance. There are four stages within the reactive wave because of the time needed for introspection and acceptance of the pain of transition.

During this wave, one addresses only the exterior, the veneer, and avoids any threats to deep-seated beliefs and values relative to personal worth.

Proactive (self as a part of the situation) occurs when one develops a totally new perspective on himself, on the situation, and the interaction between the two. Proactive is the Adlerian concept of self-observing and self-remembering in a social-systemic manner (Carsini, 1979). *Self-observing* is the process of being consciously aware of one's level of thought, whereas *self-remembering* is the capability to replay one's mental tape in a way that permits affirmative analysis of the values, beliefs, and perceptions contained in the level of thought and which created the subsequent behavior.

Within the Proactive wave, one truly *decides* on a mental shift in consciousness, values, beliefs, and perceptions. This level of change entails a profound transmutation of one's vision of reality. This shift in consciousness alters the fundamental ways one makes sense out of the world and interactively responds to it (Wilhelm-Buckley and Perkins, 1984, p. 58). A transformation occurs when a mental shift clicks with a meaning of "relationship to" (self as part of the situation) rather than "because of," and when one begins to explore a capacity to shift; i.e., the new meaning is successfully translated into action which is relational to the integrated into the environment. The *motivators* of this wave are:

- Accomplishment;
- Recognition; and
- Self-worth.

The output of this wave is the exploration of coordinating the self with the situation.

However, it is only at this point of readiness that one can consider breaking the veneer and begin to examine the true substance of the relation between one's deep-seated beliefs and values of self-worth, and the values of the system one lives in.

Coactive (self as instrumental in the situation) has as its motivation:

- Self-realization;
- Actualization; and
- Manifestation.

Within this wave, there is no need to be conscious about the use of power, no need to be "determined." The finiteness of influence and power is transformed into the infiniteness of empowerment. Herein, the metamorphosis occurs: one moves beyond the coordination and integration of self in the situation to coactively and consistently manage the synergy of the situation. By managing the synergy of the situation, I mean the ability to achieve totally satisfying and harmonious strategies that result in the highest good for all concerned. One is in harmony with his environment, has come to grips with things as they are, and is able to radiate that he is in harmony with other people in the symphony without giving up who he is.

For the Adlerian, this wave is the development of insight which is "understanding translated into constructive action." F. Capra (1982) defined this phenomenon as a "holistic-ecological-systems perspective" in which the situation "appears as a harmonious indivisible whole" (p. 19). This viewpoint "emphasizes the fundamental inter-relatedness and interdependency of all phenomena, and the intrinsically dynamic nature of physical reality" (Wilhelm-Buckley and Perkins, 1984, p. 58).

There are shifts in orientation between waves. As previously indicated, two major qualitative shifts in orientation occur as one moves from one wave to another. The difference in consciousness involved in the first shift–from Reactive to Proactive–is exemplified in James P. Carse's (1986) *Finite and Infinite Games*:

> There are at least two kinds of games. One could be called finite, the other infinite.
>
> A finite game is played for the purpose of winning, an infinite game for the purpose of continuing the play. (p. 3)

The unconscious commitment to play one's proper role as victim occurs in the Reactive Wave:

> There is no finite game unless the players freely choose to play it. No one can play who is forced to play.

It is an invariable principle for play, finite and infinite, that whoever plays, plays freely. Whoever must play, cannot play. (p. 3)

Each party attempts not only to increase the effectiveness of his argument and his power in the situation, but also to undermine the influence of those who oppose him.

If a finite game is to be won by someone it must come to a definitive end. It will come to an end when someone has won.

We know that someone has won the game when all the players have agreed who among them is the winner. No other condition than the agreement of the players is absolutely required in determining who has won the game.

It may appear that the approval of the spectators, of the referees, is also required in the determination of the winner. However, it is simply the case that if the players do not agree on a winner, the game has not come to a decisive conclusion–and the players have not satisfied the original purpose of playing. Even if they are carried from the field and forcibly blocked from further play, they will not consider the game ended. (p. 3)

Diagram 3.3, Finite and Infinite Perspectives on Power, illustrates the above points.

The shift in orientation from Proactive to Coactive is not clearcut; rather it resembles an inner, mental deep breath inhaled before one begins to coactively manage his personal and work environment.

Diagram 3.4, The Gay Model of Transition, illustrates the transition, and stages, waves, strategies, and outcomes as a whole. These are the stages that gay males move through on their odyssey from disempowerment to empowerment. This model evolved from the heuristic study, reading, and the results of the surveys in interviews. I have identified six stages and three waves of transition.

- The *waves* represent movement toward empowerment and are characterized by differing states of consciousness, qualitative shifts in perception.

- The three *strategies* are distinctive behaviors employed as methods to keep oneself in a particular wave and to enable oneself to move forward.
- The three *outcomes* are states of existence which result from the stage and wave one is in and the strategies one employs.

Distinctions to and definitions of the components of the model are contained in Chapter 4.

It is important to bear in mind that one seems to ebb and flow between stages. Seldom, if ever, does one move permanently and precisely from stage to stage, as has been illustrated in the diagram. It is more representational of general behaviors and feeling than of any given individual's progressions and regressions, which are unique to his singular experience (Adams, Hayes, and Hapson, 1976). For example, one may never get beyond Denial and Minimization. The pain of coming out of the closet is rarely viewed as a positive potential for growth, as illustrated in the recent deaths of celebrities who wanted to face the ultimate transition–death–rather than "come out." In the particular case of Rock Hudson, the public would not have known that he was gay had there not been a slip-up at Paris International Airport. In the confusion, he was taken to the American Hospital rather than the Pasteur Institute which awaited his arrival (Davidson, 1985, p. 25). One could say, from this example, that some gays feel "It is easier to die than to come out" (confidential interview). It is apparent that the designer Perry Ellis and the great Liberace made every effort to remain in the Denial stage even after their deaths.

Some have ended it all during the Depression and Victimization stage, which is all too often the portrayal of the gay lifestyle by Hollywood. Yet, some "victims," for example, may not have had the necessary support systems to move to Internalization and Transformation and thus return to the Denial and Minimization stage. The stages, then, are not so much chronological description as they are a conceptual summarization of the aspects of a common phenomenological approach of gays in corporations. Even those who have attained Actualization and Manifestation may, from time to time, revert to a previous stage.

DIAGRAM 3.3. Finite and Infinite Perspectives on Power

THE FINITE PERSPECTIVE	THE INFINITE PERSPECTIVE
Win/lose infrastructure –Scarcity thinking –A zero-sum base–100/0	Win/win infrastructure –Abundance thinking –A non-zero-sum base–100/100
Purpose is to have a winner and a loser	Purpose is to have a winner and a winner

Foundation is fear
–invokes defensiveness of
  self and purpose
	Foundation is relationship
	–invokes collaboration with
	  supportiveness and encourage-
	  ment

"Agent-orientation"–a concern for oneself as an individual	"Communal-orientation"–a concern for one's relationship to others
Strength and self-reliance equal success	Interdependence and expressed emotions equal success
Difference is right/wrong or good/bad	Difference is valued and appreciated

Strategies of choice are
finitely powerful:
–Coercive (fear)
–Expert (experience or degrees)
–Information (fact and informa-
  tion)
–Role (position and title)
–Reward (Goods/services/money
  needed by others)
	Strategy of choice is
	infinitely powerful:
	–Referent (personal worth,
	  integrity, and trust)

Operate *within* the rules to avoid censure by legitimate authority (Conventional ethics)	Operate *with* the rules to ensure the highest good for all concerned (Postconventional ethics)
Support adaptability, dis- courage creativity	Encourage creativity, support adaptability
Must include the infinite perspective	Can and generally does include the finite perspective in support of the infinite perspective
A freely chosen perspective	A freely chosen perspective

DIAGRAM 3.4. The Gay Model of Transition

STAGE	WAVE	STRATEGY	OUTCOME
I. Denial and Minimization	REACTIVE Self as a result of the situation	C O P I N G	Situationally Dependent
II. Retreat and Isolation			
III. Anger and Conflict			
IV. Depression and Victimization			
V. Internalization and Transformation	PROACTIVE Self as a part of the situation	D E A L I N G	Integration of Self in Situation
VI. Actualization and Manifestation	COACTIVE Self as instrumental in the situation	M A N A G I N G	Synergy of Self and Situation

Other researchers have developed similar models with different themes, topics, and subjects. Although my model was developed independently, I drew upon the well-known works of psychologists Adams, Hayes, Hapson, and Elisabeth Kübler-Ross to expand and refine it.

The model in the book *Transition*, (Adams, Hayes, and Hapson, 1976) was developed to describe and understand the professional development of postgraduate students in the Organizational Behaviors program at Case Western Reserve University, Cleveland, Ohio. The seven transition phases focused on self-esteem changes during transitions. The seven phases were: Immobilization; Minimization; Depression; Acceptance of Reality and Letting Go; Testing; Search for Meaning; and Internalization.

Elisabeth Kübler-Ross (1969) in *Death and Dying* charted out a very similar model of the reaction cycle people experience upon learning they are terminally ill. The phases were denial, anger, bargaining, depression, and acceptance.

Adams' and Ross's models were where the primary developmental strategies were examined. However, other developmental models that were examined were:

- Carl Jung's developmentally determined dimension of psychological growth and interjecture from the extroversion of youth to the introversion of adulthood (1971);
- Lawrence Kohlberg's theory of ethical development which suggests an invariable sequence of stages: preconventional (self-centered); conventional (avoid disapproval); and postconventional (universal ethical principles orientation) (1969);
- Roger Walsh and Frances Vaughan's six common elements of transcendence: ethics; attentional training; emotional transformation; motivation; refining awareness; and wisdom (1993);
- Stephen Covey's study of the habits of effective people: private victories of: being proactive; beginning with the end in mind; and putting first things first; public victories of: thinking win/win; seeking first to understand, then to be understood; and creative cooperation; and renewal strategies of: balanced self-renewal and working inside-out (1989); and
- Kathryn Cramer's personal change dynamics: challenge (opportunities vs. dangers); empowerment (exploration and invention) and transformation (enhancement) (1990).

As previously stated, William Bridges (1986) addressed the issue from the angle of managing organizational transitions. Bridges describes feelings of loss during transitions as having three aspects–Disengagement, Disidentification, and Disenchantment.

Karen Wilhelm-Buckley and Dami Perkins (1984) present a seven-state cycle illustrating the complexity of organizational transformation. In their transition cycle the stages are: Unconsciousness; Awakening; Reordering; Translation; Commitment; Embodiment; and Integration.

Tuckerman (1965), Bion (1961), Bennis and Shepard (1956), Gibb and Gibb (1955), and others who have studied team development have illustrated various four-stage programs: individuals, collectives, groups, and teams.

In current theories of adult development, Eric Erikson (1959) describes the "identity crisis" in adolescence. Gail Sheahy (1974) details *Passage,* and Daniel Levinson et al. (1978), gives us *The Seasons of a Man's Life.*

James Fowler describes a six-stage model for the development of Faith (Fowler, 1982). Peck, building on the work of Fowler, developed the four stages of spiritual growth. These stages are: chaotic, antisocial; formal, institutional; skeptic, individual; and mystic, communal. Finally, nature gives us spring, summer, fall, winter and infant, toddler, adolescent, adult, etc.

What is common in all these models, and provides verification for my model, is that the progression from one stage of consciousness to another can be segmented and described and that they are developmental. Just as people who experience in their organization, professional development, or state of health, we who choose empowerment also move through transformation stages.

Chapter 4, "This Is Where We Must Go," maps the stages of gay transitions in the workplace. The specific behaviors and feelings of the individuals as they move through the spiral are detailed and described.

Chapter 4

This Is Where We Must Go

We shall not cease from exploration
And the end of all our exploring
Will be to arrive where we started
And know the place for the first time . . .

— T. S. Eliot

The gay manager/executive has many stages in his journey. He may pass by a stage; he may go back and forth among them. He may stop at one and never resume his traveling. He may, and many have, successfully negotiate the whole, difficult spiral-way and in the end, like Odysseus, reach home.

I have identified six stages of transition between disempowerment and empowerment. Four describe behaviors and perceptions within the wave of Reaction–Denial and Minimization; Retreat and Isolation; Anger and Conflict; and Depression and Victimization. When an individual moves out of the Reactive wave into Proactive, the stage is characterized by Internalization and Transformation. The final step, Coactive, brings Actualization and Manifestation.

The odyssey for the gay male in the corporate world is from disempowerment to empowerment. Empowerment: What is it? What isn't it? Empowerment is not dependency or independency. Empowerment is interdependency. It calls for interdependent, coactive behaviors: behaviors in concert with the highest good of all concerned. Diagram 4.1, The Evolution of Empowerment, illustrates the evolutionary aspect of empowerment in relationship to the gay Model of Transition.

As we will see, too often, individuals view empowerment as pure independence. Not so. First, pure independence does not exist. Especially in the workplace, we are interdependent upon each other. Second, independence translates in the corporate world as adolescent, self-centered behavior. Diagram 4.2, Interdependence Is Adulthood Is Empowerment, illustrates this point.

With adulthood comes the understanding that adult-to-adult behavior empowers everyone. Any other interactions, such as adult-to-child or child-to-adult, sets up a disempowering interaction for all concerned. Misdirected anger is either adult-to-child or child-to-adult. All too often extreme activism is not coactive activism but simply misdirected anger that is disempowering for all concerned.

Transactional Analysis (TA), developed in the late 1950s by psychiatrist Eric Berne, described empowering and disempowering interactions as "transaction," which consists of three ego states–the Adult, the Parent, and the Child (Berne, 1966).

Diagram 4.3, Empowerment and TA, illustrates the principle of interaction and empowerment. The point here is that the adult-to-adult interactions in the corporate world are empowering. All other interactions, regarding homosexuality and workplace, are disempowering. This is where we must go!

However, adult-to-adult interactions require discipline, a much maligned word these days. Discipline, according to *Webster's New Collegiate Dictionary,* is: "training that corrects, molds, or perfects the mental faculties or moral character."

Covey defines discipline as:

> Discipline derives from disciple–disciple to a philosophy, disciple to a set of principles, disciple to a set of values, disciple to an overriding purpose, to a superordinate goal or a person who represents that goal.
>
> In other words, if you are an effective manager of your self, your discipline comes from within; it is a function of your independent will. You are a disciple, a follower, of your own deep values and their source. And you have the will, the integrity, to subordinate your feelings, your impulses, your moods to those values. (Covey, 1989, p.148)

Therefore, the journey from disempowerment to empowerment is adult-to-adult, interdependent behavior. This requires discipline;

DIAGRAM 4.1. The Evolution of Empowerment

THE EVOLUTION OF EMPOWERMENT

THE GAY MODEL OF TRANSITION   **EMPOWERMENT**

COACTIVE
Self as instrumental
in the solution

EMPOWERMENT/
INTERDEPENDENT

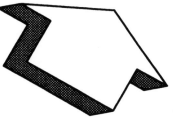

PROACTIVE
Self as part of
the solution

SELF-ACCOUNTABLE/
INDEPENDENT

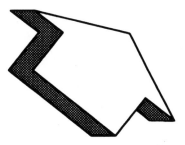

REACTIVE
Self as a result
of the solution

DISEMPOWERMENT/
DEPENDENT/
CODEPENDENT

DIAGRAM 4.2. Interdependence Is Adulthood Is Empowerment

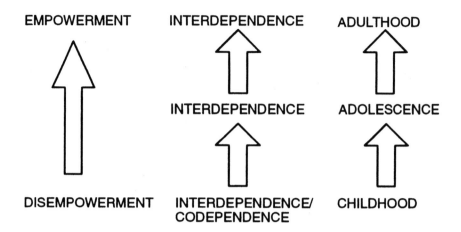

being a disciple to the wholeness and integrity of homosexuality and subordinate impulses to react other than as an adult.

In the corporate world, empowerment means to interdependently share power to increase autonomy and trust throughout the organization. It means giving everyone, gay or straight, the legitimate right to be ontologically who they are.

In this chapter I have focused on empowerment as interdependence: this is where we must go. In Chapter 5, "On the Road," under Take Personal Responsibility for Achieving the Vision, other ramifications of empowerment and specific empowering strategies and behaviors are detailed.

Given the need for a state of empowerment, enablers, factors that support and assist, need to be examined. What enables some to take up the journey, move ahead, and arrive at a state of empowerment? There seem to be four major factors which assist the individual through the various stages of the transition from disempowerment to empowerment.

The enablers are:

• Introspection and meditation;
• Creative visualization and active imagination;

• Personal responsibility and autonomy; and
• Role models and support groups.

Adams, Hayes, and Hapson's (1976) research indicated an incorrect but clear vision/expection; cognitive flexibility, i.e., low dogmatism; and a keen sense of a higher purpose enable the subjects of their study to move forward.

Clarity demands that empowerment and the enablers be outlined above but discussed in detail in Chapter 5, "On the Road." Now, let us turn to a discussion of the stages of the transition.

STAGES OF TRANSITION

I. Denial and Minimization (Reactive Wave)

Finding himself to be different from the majority of those around him, the gay male's first reaction tends to be to deny that being gay will make any difference. "My sexual preference has nothing to do with my competence. I'm good at what I do, and I don't have to deal with the gay issue in my work environment." There is a surface validity to his rationalization. The professional self and the personal self are different and can be compartmentalized. The "gay stuff" is to be dealt with at home; the "work stuff" is separate and kept at the office. As one gay accountant stated:

> Listen, you better believe I keep it a secret. Discretion is the name of the game. Anyone who doesn't know this is a fool. I isolate my life from my work. I don't mix on any kind of social level with fellow managers. Too much socialization with them could be dangerous. If I keep my business and personal life separate, so will the company. I do a damn good job here and that is all that counts. (confidential interview)

The above premise is false.

> Gay men's efforts to desexualize are in fact efforts to heterosexualize. (Woods and Lucas, 1993, p. 69)

DIAGRAM 4.3. Empowerment and TA

How We Interact with Three Ego States

(A) **Adult:**

- is the part of you that figures things out by looking at the facts.
- is your "computer"; uses facts to communicate on an adult-to-adult level.

(P) **Parent is that part of you that can be:**

- critical, or
- helping, or both.

(C) **Child is that part of you that can be:**

- naturally fun and creative, or
- stubborn and "childish."

Types of Transaction

- **EMPOWERING**

  –Adaptive:

  Complementary–message sent from a particular ego state evokes appropriate ego state response.

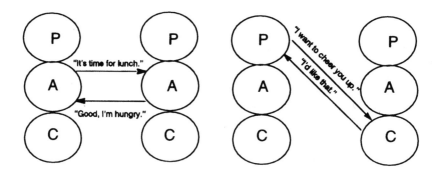

- **DISEMPOWERING**
  –Maladaptive:
  Crossed–a communicator receives a response from and/or to an inappropriate ego state.

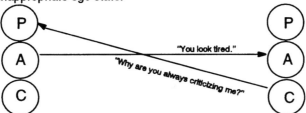

- **DISEMPOWERING**
  –Ulterior–involves two ego states and/or responses and two different messages.

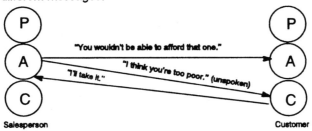

- **DISEMPOWERING**
  –Contamination: Adult becomes contaminated by his parent and/or child and thus causes mixed/crossed communication.

EMPOWERING	DISEMPOWERING		
Uncontaminated Adult	Adult Contaminated by Parent	Adult Contaminated by Child	Adult Contaminated by Both Parent & Child

- **DISEMPOWERING**
  –Exclusion: One or two states determine a person's predominant, constant communication style, for example, being a "child" in communicating.

The workplace is indeed a sexual place. One cannot get away from it. James Woods and Jay Lucas, in *The Corporate Closet*, address this issue head-on with the concept of "The Asexual Imperative."

> Our most powerful metaphor for the workplace is the machine, a comparison that encourages us to judge organizations according to their efficiency, productivity, and the smoothness of their output. We imagine that work is a rational activity and that workplaces depend on order. Sexuality, in contrast, is perceived as a threat to all that is rational and ordered, the antithesis of organization. (Woods and Lucas, 1993, p. 33)

We are not "wheels" in the machine, regardless of what corporate America would like to believe. The asexual imperative requires people to act as if they are not human beings. When it comes to homosexuality, the asexual imperative is enforced as we discussed in Chapter 2, "This Is Where We Are."

As long as pictures of the spouse and children appear on the desk of heterosexuals, the workplace will be sexual. Because business is done by humans and not machines, business consists of human actions, reactions, and relationships. As addressed in Chapter 2, this "asexual myth" thinking is a Catch-22. Organizations speak "as if" they were asexual but covertly act sexually.

Talking about pictures on the desk, Louie Crew, in his study of university English chairpersons stated:

> Only a member of the ruling class could enjoy the luxury of saying, "I am no more concerned with the sex life of my faculty that I am with what brand of underwear they wear, and I would consider their flaunting of either in equally bad taste." The key here is the word *flaunting*. The heterosexual dictators of our culture have so defined our way of life that heterosexual references to one's wife, husband, children, even in the most academic of settings, are not considered *flaunting*; yet let a gay professor just quietly place a picture of her wife or his husband on the desk in the office like anyone else . . . . (Crew, 1978, p. 19)

As long as there are relationships the workplace will be sexual. Psychologically, there is no such thing as asexual. The asexual imperative is not real for heterosexuals and is a trap for gays.

David Rothenberg offers an argument against this asexual myth.

> Someone recently commented to me that gays keep announc-
> ing what they do in bed. He then asked, "Wouldn't it be
> embarrassing for heterosexuals to do the same?" Another
> myth. I never tell anyone what I do in bed when I state that I
> am gay. When a candidate for office parades wife and children
> into a TV commercial, he is "coming out" to me as a hetero-
> sexual. When a man nibbles on a woman's ear in the seat in
> front of me at a theater, he is "coming out" while "coming
> on." (Rothenberg, 1979, *Gayweek*, p. 19)

Vito Russo stated:

> When I say my brother and his wife are heterosexual, that
> doesn't mean I'm talking about their sex lives. Likewise, when
> we say someone is gay, we're talking about *sexual orientation*,
> not their sexual activity. It's not our fault that every time
> someone says "gay," people think "sex." That's *their* twisted
> problem. (Russo, 1990, *Village Voice,* p. 4)

Communication about sex, in corporations, is repressed to pictures
on the desk (How did the kids get there?) or the ludicrous jokes.

In other words, it is not the act of sex itself that is being examined, but our reaction to it. The present reaction is "binary logic" (Woods and Lucas, 1993, p. 37). Binary logic is reflected in the
logic of the gay account above. Gay-stuff equals home. Profession-
al-stuff equals work. This is not reality. It minimizes one's integrity
and ontological goodness of being gay and denies the reality of the
workplace as sexual.

> Yet for all their eagerness to detach sexuality from work and to
> distinguish the sexual (and superficial) from the personal (and
> essential), gay men find the task a difficult one. Personal and
> professional roles are firmly entwined, the reason for this
> largely beyond their control: Work is a social activity. (Woods
> and Lucas, 1993, p. 21)

Furthermore, frequent explicit and implicit sexual stories and conversations serve as the infrastructure of trust. When one withholds

information about his sexuality (not sex), he is not building trust and thereby places limits on the growth of a business relationship.

All this is to say that believing that the workplace is asexual or acting as if your work and your homosexuality are separate is reactive. Reactive is to be in a state of denial. If the gay male adheres to the "asexual imperative," he is caught in the Reactive Wave of denial of reality and minimization of the impact of his homosexuality.

Herein, the Reactive Wave coping strategies are employed. "Coping" is defined as behaviors that maintain. They are not behaviors that permit resolution of issues, of the possibility of movement. The basic coping behaviors exhibited by the individual are conformity and going along with the status quo. He may conform to ensure survival and security; he may strive to do more work than expected in the hope of gaining acceptance. Often, one devalues his own abilities and potential, granting greater knowledge and expertise to others, usually straight, powerful men. Enormous amounts of energy are spent sensing out and being tuned into "the other." For many, this Denial stage goes on throughout their careers, a lifelong pattern of functional schizophrenic (split). It is this stage that perpetuates the dark closets of corporate America.

The metaphor "in-the-closet" or "out-of-the-closet" is the principal image used to communicate one's existence by our gay community. It is my belief that the metaphor whether one is "in" or "out" connotes how disempowered we gays are. We never have positive, empowered metaphors in our descriptive language. Be that as it may, "in-the-closet" involves making oneself, for whatever reasons, a "person-of-the-lie," masquerading–presenting oneself as being just like the homosexual majority, by throwing into and hiding in the closet whatever evidence exists to the contrary.

Closets are dark and musty places where one places and hides things from common view. They are too cramped and oppressive for living. Yet, the majority of gay managers and executives in this study have chosen to live there. One reinforcement of this is the erroneous premise that the workplace should be asexual. On the other hand, there are some who survived hostility and discrimination, believing the Pacific Northwest saying "Rough winters make for good timber." There are the gays who are not in the Reactive Wave. They have achieved the best of both, in that they have achieved and succeeded at being a gay manager or executive without being a person of the lie.

It is here (Denial and Minimization–Reactive Wave) that the self-veiling begins. The persona-mask is put on and put on tightly. The gay male begins to become a person who plays a role. He plays "parts" within a limited, self-imposed boundary in a schizophrenic (split) manner which helps him and others avoid dealing with the "whole." Only later, if ever, does the reality of all the years of "self-veiling" become apparent to him. It is then that he realizes what the philosopher Hegel addressed so often in his works: that the cumulative effect of a lifetime of substitution of a "part" of the whole for the "whole" leads to an unbearable lack of authenticity and integrity. If the individual recognizes this dearth, he can begin the bittersweet process of "unveiling," which occurs during the Internalization and Transformation stage.

A point is reached when it is understood that denial will no longer work. The perceptive gay male realizes that the workplace is not asexual, and learns that the ability to move up in the corporation is not based entirely upon competence. The advancement of his career is partly dependent on how well he develops relationships with those in power around him. Whether his superiors and colleagues view him in a positive way is a very subjective–but crucially pivotal–element in his career advancement. Those in power demonstrably tend to favor others just like themselves–white, family men, etc., as discussed in Chapter 2.

Some gays experience a sense of being overwhelmed with the reality that their lifestyle will be a consideration, and more often a negative consideration, by the corporation. At this point of "closet-maintenance," some may resort to a web of lies or, at best, half-truths in an attempt to pass, to maintain the safety of the closet as they perceive it. *Truth is the first sacrifice made in order to belong.*

Woods and Lucas label this behavior as "counterfeiting."

> The term counterfeit is useful in this context because it stresses the active nature of the task, distinguishing it from strategies that permit the performer to be passive. (Woods and Lucas, 1993, p. 75)

In other words, the person is "passing." Passing is a play within which one puts on a persona-mask, that is, the public face is just a performance. Some choose not to lie, but their silence becomes noticeable. Conformance is still the norm. Richard Zoglin (1979) reports an interview which illustrates what can happen to Truth:

> However, few executives can avoid the subject of their private life completely and when it comes up, gay businessmen must decide how far they will go to cover up their homosexuality. The director of data processing for a paper manufacturing company says that his associates assume it's with a girl. "When I talk about what I did over the weekend I tell the truth–I just change the personal pronoun. I will often be eating lunch with one of the vice presidents or the controller or somebody," he continues, "and the talk will get to sex–as it always does. I will play along. For example, when we comment on girls, they all know what 'my type' is." He has devised a nice rationalization to help him live with his deception: "I probably would sleep with a woman if I got the chance and there are certain kinds of women who appeal to me more than others–so I'm really not lying when I talk about my type." (pp. 71-72)

One of the primary coping mechanisms during the Denial stage is minimization. The gay male will project an image of "I don't care," which all too often is simply a false mask, a state of contrived euphoria. While the mask is being worn, the psyche is saying, "This is not actually happening," or "This won't actually affect me." Like the inhabitants of Plato's cave, he sits in dark alcoves watching shadows that he mistakes for reality!

It is at this stage that one feels most vulnerable and powerless due to a perceived lack of control over one's own destiny. By the time the gay male has entered the workforce, he has a long history of being rejected or punished for being gay. His anxiety is from being unable to cope with the consequences of not going along, e.g., perhaps fired or "exposed" as being a "faggot." It is therefore understandable that he may masochistically stay closeted. That pain, sadly, is more acceptable than the pain of rejection and abandonment.

During interviews, individuals describe their anxiety as fear of rejection, followed by the fear of having to face such undesirable responses as anger or punishment. Rosenfels (1971) points out this blockage to development as common in the beginning stages.

> The search for personal importance rests on the development of an inner identity and involves the individual in a growth struggle which has painful and disturbing qualities. It is easy to believe that thinking what you are supposed to think and doing what you are supposed to do in a structured civilized world will bring a fulfilled sense of individuality. The more the individual adapts himself to the more institutionalized demands of society, the more he becomes aware of the essential emptiness of the kind of life. (p. 9)

Keen (1983) addresses rejection from the angle of child-rearing practices and masochistic behavior.

> Hence, when a baby is bonded to cruel parents, it comes to associate the only kind of conditional love and security it has with the pain it receives. To the abused child, painfully bonded, the motto of life becomes the dreadful choice Faulkner posed at the end of "The Old Man": ". . . between nothingness and grief, I will choose grief, I will choose grief." The masochist returns to pain because it is psychologically linked to the only security he knew as a child. It is better to be punished than be ignored. Pain becomes the perverse signal that somebody cares. (p. 54)

It was my personal experience, and that of over 80 percent whom I interviewed, that coming to grips with our sexuality and coming out was pain equal to abandonment.

Bear in mind, the Denial-Minimization stage falls within the Reactive Wave (self as result of the situation). The individual is not ready or willing to see himself as a contributor to the situation, as the above behaviors indicate. It is also important to note that Denial and Minimization is a common stage in the process of transition. It is a normal and necessary psychic reaction to a crisis which is too frightening to face head-on (Adams, Hayes, and Hapson, 1976; Kübler-Ross, 1969). This stage provides time to get ready to process this new, profound perception and overcome feelings of vulnerability.

II. *Retreat and Isolation (Reactive Wave)*

In the Retreat and Isolation stage, gays allow the reality of their situation to penetrate their closeted thinking. They feel removed from the mainstream and are acutely aware of being "different" from the others around them. They come to understand that they are functioning from a frame of reference that is different from the heterosexuals.

This is a stage of immobilization or being "frozen-up." Gays retreat in order to try to make sense out of what is happening. A shift in perception–that they contribute to and are a part of the situation–has not occurred. Therefore, they flounder in the waves.

Those interviewed stated a sense of being unintentionally a cog in the wheel. They continued to be involved in an approach-avoidance mechanism. The social approach was to calmly proceed at work as if their lifestyle had neither a positive nor a negative impact on their work and working relationships. The avoidance occurred when their fellow workers did not respond likewise. It became a vicious cycle of approach, avoid; approach, avoid, etc.

After such experiences, these men reported a feeling of being unable to cope effectively with the relationships and climate of the work environment.

Coping behavior, i.e., "closet maintenance," is continued. Nuances are added. The coping behavior exhibited by the individual is isolation, ranging from physically setting one's self apart from others to total abstention from interpersonal communications and alliances. One individual reported that he would only use the restroom facilities when he knew no one was in there or likely to come in. His rationale was one of fear of being accused of flirtation or "cruising the men's room" if he spoke to someone in the restroom (confidential interview).

Helplessness and powerlessness characterize feelings regarding relationships and climate in the workplace. This stage is also within the Reactive Wave (self as a result of the situation). And once again, the individual does not yet have the capacity or the motivation to examine how he is contributing to his own disempowerment.

It is important to note that in this stage gay males continue a behavior characteristic of the Denial and Minimization stage. They focus their energies on the task of the work itself. Striving to do more than expected and to be better than others becomes their goal. The fallacy lies in the assumption that this behavior will gain them acceptance and credibility from the corporation. In over 90 percent of the reported cases, it simply brought more work.

Individuals in the Retreat and Isolation stage feel they are being "quarantined" and being "punished because I'm good!" One gay publishing executive reported:

> For three years I busted my ass around there. I was the kind of guy who came in early and left late. Leaving late is not the word for it. Many a night I didn't get out of the office until after midnight trying to get the best damn proposal for the company. I work hard being a Superman manager. One day I was in the hallway and overheard my VP saying to one of my peers, "You know _____ has got another think coming if he thinks he's going to get that promotion. Jane saw him down at that fag bar, you know." (confidential interview)

Sadly, this individual simply went to another and then another corporation repeating the stages of Denial and Minimization, Retreat and Isolation because he accepted a myth of commonly held assumptions, addressed earlier, which are not questioned by the majority of those living within the system.

It is at this stage that those who are able to see alternative courses of action tend to leave corporations, seek other career paths, or move into managing, dealing, or coping strategies.

III. Anger and Conflict (Reactive Wave)

Anger and Conflict is the eruption stage. Internal and external "storming" begins to occur: emotional response to task demands and relationship behavior becomes one of anger and hostility. One has stopped denying to himself that he is gay. He has stopped denying that his life-style, in and of itself–regardless of who he is and his competence level–interrupts his work environment and career. It is now apparent that the corporation expects to exert a certain amount of control over the way in which he lives his life. This creates resentment.

Once again, because this stage is in the Reactive Wave (self as a result of the situation), gay men do not see they are giving up their own power and control through the use of anger and conflict. Usually this awareness comes through models and gay support systems, within which gays at this stage tend not to be involved.

During interviews, persons in this stage and those who reflected back to this stage of inward anger ("Why me?" or "I don't deserve this!" or similar statements), indicated that they felt insulated and "endangered" by the corporation.

These feelings are generated by the recognition that the perceived quid pro quo for conformance has not been forthcoming–the gay glass ceiling. These feelings are then translated into external defense behaviors.

Recall that in this Reactive Wave, individuals are acting out of "deficiency motivation." The behaviors exhibited are protest, blaming and rejection of "the others" and, in most cases, the corporation's espoused standards. The desired effect is to produce change and achieve relief. Frequent references are made to the way things should be, and disparities between formal and informal policies and practices are exposed. As reported by a first level manager in a telecommunications firm:

> Let me tell you, every day is an endless battle. I come in to work and swear my boss got up in the morning, looked in the mirror and said, "How can I screw over _____ today."
>
> What he usually did was dig up some policy that I've violated, then pile work on. Well, I've learned. Now, even the looks I give him when he comes in warn him! (confidential interview)

The conflicts that ensue begin with a type of "bargaining." The bargaining premise is: "If you would just accept me for what and who I am, and if you'd look at the good work I do, we wouldn't have any of these problems." Bargaining is an attempt by the gay individual to cut his losses, garnered by the initial hostilities, and regain control over the situation.

This coping strategy, in and of itself, places the gay in a position of powerlessness. It is akin to the teenage request, "If I do the dishes, do I get the car?" We all know how far that gets one! The one in the position of power, role-power, or the power just given them by the bargaining process, usually continues to proceed from his power base and continues the same behaviors.

Having discovered that bargaining is a powerless and humiliating position, the gay individual tends toward outright conflict. He has firmly committed himself to a particular position on the issue of his gayness and engages in conflict with the corporation resulting in a win-lose outcome. The conflict is exhibited in the traditional fight, flight, freeze syndrome.

The finite behaviors of *fight* take the form of deep, emotional altercations. For example, ideas are attacked before they are completely expressed; comments and suggestions are made with a great deal of vehemence; behavior is exhibited by hostile, facial nonverbals illustrative of inner feelings of hatred; and attacks are aimed at the personal level in very subtle ways. As reported by a gay supervisor in a telecommunications firm:

> I got real tired of his shit. He wanted everyone in his office for a meeting now! So I got everybody in the damn building to show up. Even the maintenance folks came. (confidential interview)

The *flight* strategy is usually employed after a series of prolonged, "winless" altercations. The finite behavior of flight takes the form of internal escape. The individual avoids entanglement, fleeing behind a barrage of stories of weekend adventures. He asks questions to elicit conversation and to avoid being questioned.

The *freeze* strategy is usually employed after the fight and flight strategies have been unsuccessful. The finite behaviors of freeze take the form of passive resistance. The behavior is usually exhibited by "make me do it" verbals and nonverbals. The ultimate freeze strategy becomes to do exactly what one is told to do: "Just tell me what to do and I'll do it. (And that's all I'll do!)"

Ninety percent of those at this stage reported a sense of power based on force, strength in numbers, etc. No one came close to reporting a sense of empowerment based on inner convictions.

For many this Anger and Conflict stage goes on throughout their careers. All too often they become the warriors who provide the structure of dead bodies from which to launch the next attack. After the smoke has cleared, the bodies piled up, one feels the hopelessness and powerlessness of constant conflict.

IV. Depression and Victimization (Reactive Wave)

Depression and Victimization is the most devastating stage into which people fall. In this state, gays give up their ambitions and play the role that is required of them. They, like the well-trained pup, will lift their paw for a biscuit! They perceive themselves as locked into a situation over which they have no control. They become "stuck" in their careers and lose any expectation of significant advancement. People in such a position become disengaged, feel a lower level of commitment to their work, and even withdraw from responsibility.

This stage brings to a culmination the Reactive Wave (self as a result of the situation). Herein, the gay individual feels totally powerless. The realities of the negative impact that his life-style has upon the organization and the resulting stresses become apparent to him.

> As people become aware that they must make some changes in the way they are living, as they become aware of the realities involved, they begin to get depressed . . . . They become depressed because they are just beginning to face up to the fact that there has been a change. Even if they have voluntarily created this change themselves there is likely to be this dip in feelings. They become frustrated because it becomes difficult to know how best to cope with the new life requirements, the ways of being, the new relationships that have been established or whatever other changes may be necessary. (Adams, Hayes, and Hapson, 1976, p. 11)

Feelings of powerlessness and hurt are generated by the recognition that the desired acceptance and recognition have not been forthcoming. Rather, their deepest fears of abandonment, rejection, and punishment have been realized.

Feelings of victimization arise out of a sense of injury which occurred during altercations; the sense of powerlessness arises from the fallacy that "the other" is in control, and things can get better only if "the other" changes. To understand that there is no persecutor unless there is a willing victim is beyond the emotional and rational capability of the "victim" at this stage of the finite game. Such understanding requires a mental and capacity shift in beliefs and behaviors which occurs in another stage.

In the stage of Depression and Victimization the individual does nothing to change the behaviors exhibited in this stage and nothing to help himself. Tasks are completed in an acceptable manner and relationships are cordial and kept to a minimum. The individual exists in a state of "the walking wounded," proceeding without a sense of self-worth or expectations of advancement.

Sadly, many at this stage begin to identify with their "captors" much in the way that "hostage phenomena" work. As reported by a gay manager in a head-hunting firm:

> Hey! It's okay. I came through all this discrimination to understand that they are the ones with the power. Sure you can cause a lot of stink. You may even get what you think you wanted. However, they win in the long run by shelving you in some dead-end position. (confidential interview)

This stage provides the psychic readiness and willingness to continue on toward other stages. But many do not continue the pilgrimage toward empowerment. It is no longer devoted. The pain of the victim is often more comfortable than the pain of self-examination and introspection that the next stage will require. Perhaps M. Scott Peck (1978) truly knew what he was talking about when he addressed the issue of self-exploration and growth by titling his book *The Road Less Traveled*.

V. Internalization and Transformation (Proactive Wave)

This stage begins the second wave of transformation from disempowerment to empowerment. The behaviors exhibited up until now have been generated by needs for survival, security, belonging, and the "deficiency motivation." The strategies have been coping strategies. The focus has been the self as a result of the situation. The outcome is one of situational dependency.

It is at this point that the individual chooses to look *inside* in a quest that moves *outside* and *beyond*, but not against the self or the corporation. Sam Keen (1983) relates this inward quest to outlaw behavior. Outlaws peel back the layers of self-veiling.

> To become an outlaw, I must stand out, dare to become a first person singular, refuse to take refuge in the corporate "we." I must turn inside-out, become inner-directed rather than outer-directed. I must turn my back on the consensus and begin an inner journey into the unknown interior, the terra incognita of my self. The adventure is inward bound–the discovery of the nature of consciousness. (p. 132)

Herein, the individual begins to turn away from the persona, the mask, and toward self. Herein, the individual dares to face his own projections and thereby acknowledge his unconscious needs and conscious behaviors which characterized previous stages. As Pogo said, "We have met the enemy and he is us." Herein, the individual wins a new freedom only after the agonizing process of transformation. Herein, the individual comes to the realization that the path to empowerment involves the painful knowledge of how one has disempowered oneself.

It is at this point that one realizes that the trauma of the Reactive Wave is not where one wants to stay. It is here that the awareness of the situation has the prospect of challenge as well as the prospect of threat. Kathryn Cramer, in her book *Staying on Top,* presents a model that indicates that in any stressful situation one has two mental options–challenge (opportunities and gains) or threat (dangers and losses). Diagram 4.4, Dynamic Model of Traumatic Change, illustrates Cramer's point.

> Remember, in any stressful situation the prospect of *challenge* is just as real as the prospect of *threat,* even though you may not readily be able to identify the challenges. The challenges will become apparent when you find in your trauma the opportunities that exist alongside the dangers. When you are able to see both, they will be distinct focal points: positive aspects that foster *challenge* and negative factors that spawn *threat.* (Cramer, 1990, p. 117)

Internalization because of introspection helps one to understand the vital role perception plays in the journey. Staying in the Reactive

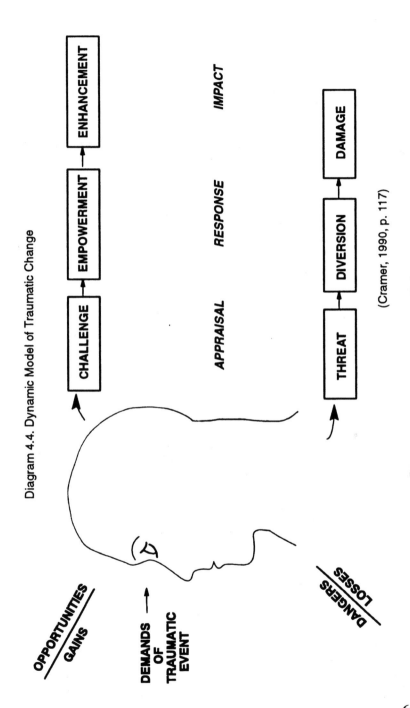

Diagram 4.4. Dynamic Model of Traumatic Change

(Cramer, 1990, p. 117)

Wave is to act out of fear. Paralyzed, the individual only sees "danger and losses." Sadly, it becomes self-fulfilling. In spite of what those in this wave would say, it eventually leads to what Cramer calls "Damage." Damage to integrity and wholeness. It is choosing neurotic suffering in a feeble attempt to avoid existential suffering.

However, accepting existential suffering and doing one's inner work is a choice to focus on "opportunities and gains" of continuing the odyssey from disempowerment to empowerment (see Diagram 4.5). Put simply, the old adage "Is the glass half empty or half full?" is what we are discussing. Perceiving it as half empty is a choice to focus on "losses."

Once one has crossed the bridge between the Reactive Wave and the Proactive Wave, an acceptance of the reality of being a gay male in a heterosexual, male-dominated corporation occurs. This is an acceptance of reality for what it is, rather than a fantasy of "what it should be." For this capacity shift to happen, a process of unhooking from the attachment of the past occurs.

> To move . . . involves a process of unhooking from the past and of saying, "Okay, here I am now; here is what I have; here's what I want." As this is accepted as the new reality, the person's feelings begin to rise once more, and optimism becomes possible. A clear "letting go" is necessary. (Adams, Hayes, and Hapson, 1976, p. 12)

"Letting go" permits one to become more involved with who he is and how he interacts in work relationships. He starts testing himself within this new situational perception, trying on the new suit of empowerment and new ways of dealing with and molding situations. The word "empowerment" now has the internalized definition of "enabled"–enabled through a process of internal leveling and centering, or, as Paul Tillich (1952) said, "in spite of" but "interactive with" the environment.

> The courage to be is the courage to affirm our own rational nature, in spite of everything in us that conflicts with its union with the rational nature of being-itself . . . . (p. 13);

Diagram 4.5. The Gay Model of Transition and the Dynamic Model of Traumatic Change

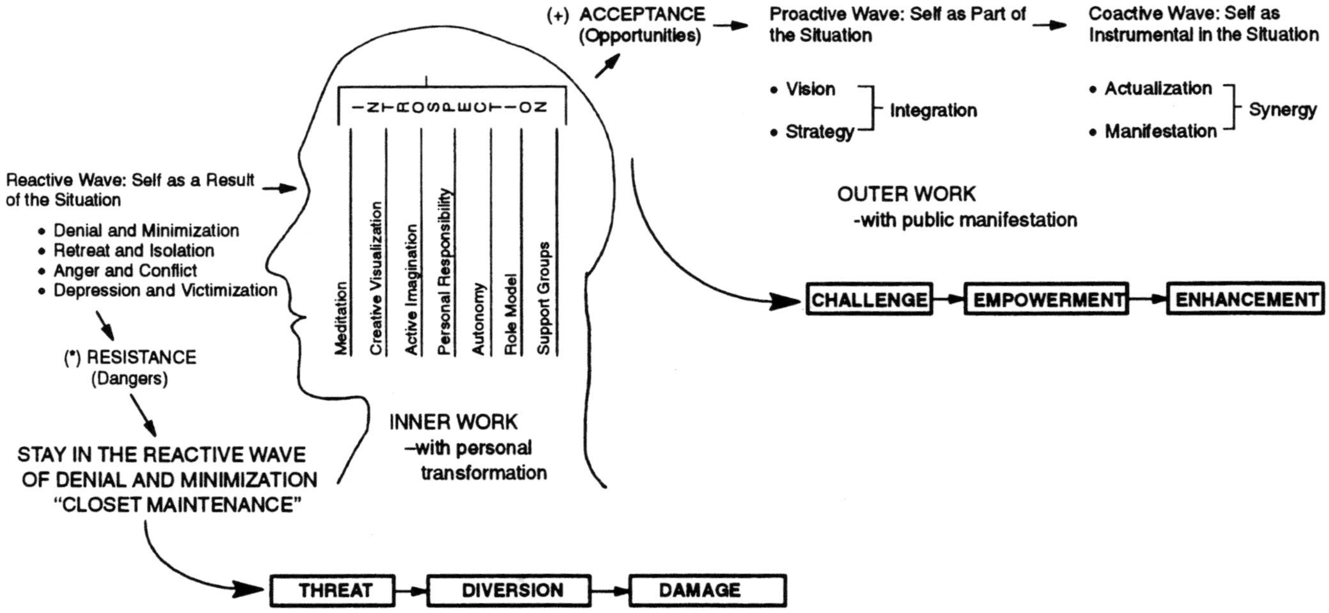

Reactive Wave: Self as a Result of the Situation

- Denial and Minimization
- Retreat and Isolation
- Anger and Conflict
- Depression and Victimization

(*) RESISTANCE (Dangers)

STAY IN THE REACTIVE WAVE OF DENIAL AND MINIMIZATION "CLOSET MAINTENANCE"

(+) ACCEPTANCE (Opportunities)

TRANSITION

Meditation
Creative Visualization
Active Imagination
Personal Responsibility
Autonomy
Role Model
Support Groups

INNER WORK -with personal transformation

Proactive Wave: Self as Part of the Situation

- Vision
- Strategy

] Integration

OUTER WORK -with public manifestation

Coactive Wave: Self as Instrumental in the Situation

- Actualization
- Manifestation

] Synergy

CHALLENGE → EMPOWERMENT → ENHANCEMENT

THREAT → DIVERSION → DAMAGE

67

The courage to be is not one thing beside others. It is an expression of the essential act of everything that participates in being . . . . (p. 20);

Courage can meet every object of fear, because it is an object and makes participation possible. (p. 26).

The motivators in this stage of Internalization and Transformation are:

- Self-accomplishment;
- Personal growth;
- Recognition; and
- Self-worth.

Because of these motivators, one has shifted toward becoming intently concerned with internal understanding. One seeks meaning on the cognitive level for the hows and whys of his involvement in such activities as the isolation, anger, and denial of Stages 1 through 4.

Thus, the gay is now ready and eager to peel back the veneer that was so dear to him in the Reactive Wave. Herein, he is willing to commit himself to introspection so that he can see the ineffectiveness of the strategies employed earlier. The necessary, vital inner work begins!

The feelings herein are mixed. There is fear, vulnerability, and occasional low self-esteem as risks of loss, independence, commitment, and self-confrontation are taken. "Can I do it?" and "Am I ready?" will often rear their negative, ugly heads. However, the support system one had developed and his power of creative visualization rises up. A sense of excitement and empowerment comes as the risks pay off.

The dealing behaviors exhibited during the stage of Internalization and Transformation are:

- Assessment;
- Goal determination; and
- Forward movement.

Assessment of what is in the environment and what is in the self occurs. The crucial question, "How have I contributed to the current situation?" is finally asked. Through introspection, acceptance of responsibility for the situation occurs. Diagram 4.6, Motivators and Dealing Behaviors in the Internalization and Transformation Stage, illustrates the above concept.

This stage requires clearly defining one's drives for self-accomplishment, personal growth, recognition, and self-worth; admitting these drives to one's self, giving them specific form in terms of goals and strategies, and going public, i.e., letting the boss and some others know that one is gay and enlisting their support. The behavior requires a calm, centered, assertive self-determination.

In this stage, gay persons start to develop skills in order to solve or, at least, deflect the problems they encounter. They learn to be perceptive concerning in whom it is safe to confide and in whom it

DIAGRAM 4.6. Motivators and Dealing Behaviors in the Internalization and Transformation Stage

STAGE

Internalization
and
Transformation

MOTIVATORS

- Self-accomplishment
- Personal growth
- Recognition
- Self-worth

DEALING BEHAVIORS

o Assessment
o Goal determination
o Forward movement

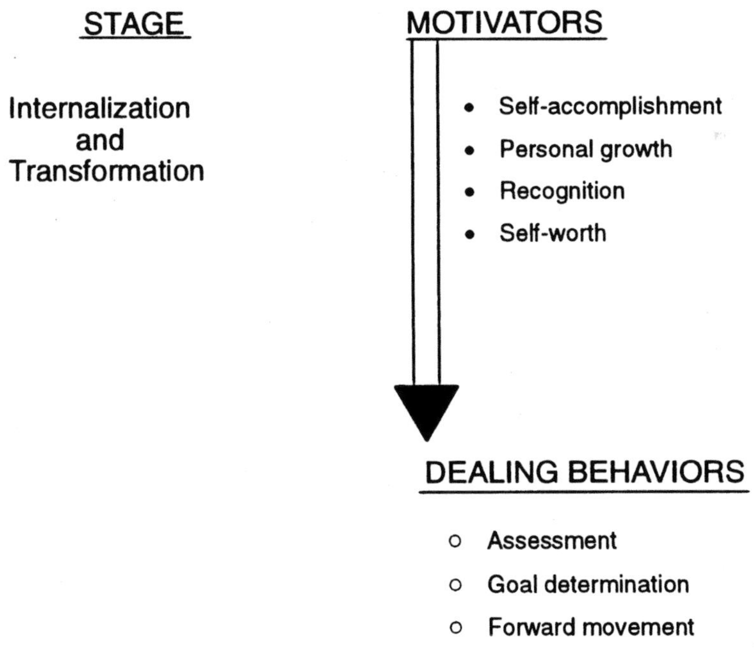

is not. They pick up on cues regarding the extent of others' knowledge of their situation and their reactions to it. They build alliances with members of the majority who are sympathetic to their position.

VI. Actualization and Manifestation (Coactive Wave)

A transformation occurs as one moves from the Internalization and Transformation stage to Actualization and Manifestation. Stage VI is in the wave of Coactive (self as instrumental in the situation). The outcome is the synergy of the self and the situation.

For synergy to occur a major transformation needs to take place. A transformational shift in consciousness, belief, values, and perceptions is needed. This mental and capacity shift entails a profound transmutation of the previous two perceptions ("self as a result of the situation" and "self as a part of the situation") to the self as an instrument of "controlling catalyst." Wilhelm-Buckley and Perkins (1984) refer to a similar process as "transformation."

> Transformation is the process of formulating a vision from the integration of information, metaphorical images, personal vision, and feelings collected in the unconscious, awakening, and reordering states. The vision evolves into a clear image of what the organization wants to achieve, which then organizes and instructs every step toward the desired future. Specific long-range goals and strategies for implementation emerge from the vision, enabling individuals to move forward in the concerted effort. (p. 62)

There is no sharp division between the Internalization-Transformation stage and Actualization. The transformation from one stage to another seems to be similar to what Bridges (1986) has called the "neutral zone."

> In the ancient rites of passage that used to carry a person through periods of transition, the neutral zone was present in a literal "nowhere." There, in the desert or forest or tundra, the person could break away from the social forces that held his or her old reality in place, and a new reality could emerge. The neutral zone wilderness was believed to be a point of closer

access to the spirits or the deeper levels of reality, and so the Plains Indians called the journey into the wilderness a "vision quest."

One does not have to accept the ancient beliefs to recognize that the neutral zone is still a place of discovery. Studies of creativity always emphasize that the creative solution comes from the psychological equivalent of the neutral zone. (p. 30)

The "neutral zone" is not a wasteland of nothingness. The Japanese have a wonderful word that depicts the "fullness" of the neutral zone described by the interviewees. The Japanese word "ma" refers to the necessary pause that one must take in anticipation of the right moment for action. The "ma" that permits that inner, mental, deep breath that artists describe as occurring seconds before creativity explodes. The Australian aborigines have a similar process called "a Walk-About!"

Gays experience their own "neutral zone." A gay bank manager describes the "ma"–that inner, mental, deep breath–before the gay individual decides to manifest, that is, to radiate who he is coactively and simultaneously with his work environment.

It was as if I have been moving in slow motion and watching myself move in slow motion, for the last few months. I knew I had been comfortable at work but something was missing. Then it suddenly hit me, that being gay didn't mean I had to walk one step behind or out of sync with everyone else. It meant being in time and playing with everyone else. And sometimes it meant getting others to play my tune, as well. (confidential interview)

Herein, managing strategies, as distinguished from coping and dealing strategies as earlier defined, are employed. *Managing* is defined as behaviors that coactively, i.e., in synergy with others, evolve. They are behaviors that permit growth rather than resolution of issues and movement in sync with one's environment. The individual gives up the illusion of being separated from his environment. Therefore, managing behaviors occur.

The Actualization stage comes with the recognition that one's disadvantaged position has fostered a deeper understanding of oneself and the development of useful skills. Being on the outside forces the individual to look inside the organization, to understand the unwritten rules and the norms of the corporate workplace. Observation skills are sharpened. The "ruling class" is often oblivious to such skills.

The gay outsider also is keenly aware that he is in a vulnerable position and learns to play out scenarios of possible future situations–problem anticipation skills. Similarly, vulnerability leads to playing one's cards closer to the vest, caution in sharing information, and more aggressiveness in seeking information. One learns, for example, to start conversations by asking questions. This approach allows one to test the waters, to explore the other's position before divulging one's own, thus developing unique probing skills and techniques.

Still another positive product of the gay's position is the development of empathy. This arises not so much because one is gay, but because one is a member of a minority. To operate in that context, gays must learn to put themselves in the shoes of the majority in order to understand how they see things. One is almost forced to be sensitized to others' viewpoints. Sadly, the majority all too often has not had to be sensitized. It is their Achilles' heel.

Self-actualization is existing in act and not merely in potentiality. It is the quality or state of being factual and authentic. It is the state within which gays experience an intensive drive for integrity, that quality of being complete and undivided from their homosexuality. They have come to recognize, deal with, and celebrate their homosexuality as an authentic element of their being and existence. Jerry Herman's 1983 Broadway musical *La Cage aux Folles* addresses the concept of actualization:

> I am what I am
> I am my own special creation
> So come take a look
> Give me the hook
> It's my world that I want to take
>   a little pride in
> My world, and it's not a place I
>   have to hide in

> Life's not worth a damn
> Till you can say, "Hey world,
>   I am what I am."

Self-actualization is a state of integrity. *Integrity* is a state of unimpaired soundness. It is the quality of being incorruptible, complete, and individual. Integrity is the unity of body (matter), mind (will), and spirit (energy) in a way that created wholeness, individuation, as well as indivisibility, so that one is synchronistically in the motion of beingness (who one is). The *motion of beingness* is to be coactively integral, i.e, that which is essential to completeness; lacking nothing essential because it is formed as a unit with other parts.

Peck comes at integrity from the angle of "paradoxical thinking" and integration.

> Thinking with integrity is paradoxical thinking. And it is not only necessary that we think with integrity, it's also necessary that we act with integrity. Behaving with integrity is "praxis" . . . . Praxis refers to the integration of your proactive with your belief system. (Peck, 1994, p. 209)

In other words, integrity is not the old argument of faith versus good actions. Integrity is the ying/yang of Taoism. Integrity is one's belief and behavior as one. *Unum.*

As addressed earlier, under existential suffering, integrity is not easy or automatic. Integrity is coming to grips with the angst of being, in this case being gay. It is all too easy (neurotic suffering) to be the counterfeiter, the person-of-the-lie, than it is to integrate one's behavior with one's belief. To be in a state of praxis is never painless but it is always ontologically peaceful, and fully empowering.

To pursue a state of integrity is to first realize that beingness and integrity are one. Integrity is not "something out there." Realizing this, the pursuit of integrity moves to being "integral" with one's environment. Denial of one's homosexuality is to shatter one's beingness and therefore one's integral part in the movement of the universe.

The managing behaviors are coactive managing behaviors that permit the harmonious motion of beingness that is totally satisfying and fulfilling for the highest good of all concerned. A state of resonance, i.e, vibrating in harmony with one's homosexuality and the environment, is achieved. Diagram 4.7 illustrates integrity. Self-actualization, being in a state of integrity, brings with it the discovery of full empoweredness.

Manifestation is the state of radiating one's empoweredness and one's integrity. It is a state of resonance. Resonance is the phenomenon of differing tones which, while maintaining their individuality, give rise to a natural, stable vibration.

In our study, very few individuals experienced a state of manifestation. Many reported what they call manifestation. However, within the constructs of this study, those experiences were more likely integration rather than manifestation.

The feelings described during the state were of being empowered–in control of one's own life rather than dependent, passive, weak, "bossed"–free of blocks, inhibitions, fears; self-determining; and with a keen sense of direct connection with one's environment.

Those who attempt to exist at this Olympian level no longer conceive of their need for independence and their commitment to work, their profession, and their corporation as conflicting forces. Instead, interdependence, individuation, and commitment to the organization, its mission, its products and services, are experienced as integrated aspects of task and working relationships.

This peak of Actualization and Manifestation can be conceived of as the Reactive Wave: self as a result of the situation, turned inside out.

What has to be negotiated by the empowered gay and his organization is the *task to be engaged in*–not his need for survival, security, belonging, accomplishment, recognition, and self-worth.

> The treasurer of a national hotel chain received an anonymous phone call saying, "Your assistant treasurer is a fag." The gay assistant treasurer recalls how his boss came to him disturbed and cautiously said he wanted to ask a question. Before he finished, I said, "Yes, I'm homosexual. Now what else important do you want to ask me?" The treasurer was somewhat taken aback by his casualness but he was relieved–and their working relationship had not been affected. (Zoglin, 1979, p. 73)

DIAGRAM 4.7. Model of Integrity

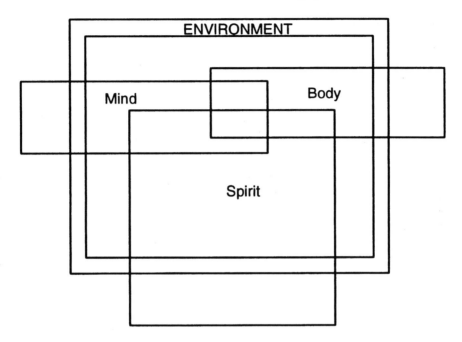

The assistant treasurer disarmed his enemy by re-owning the propaganda. This strategy can only be performed by one who has traveled the journey from disempowerment to empowerment.

With empowerment, the level of relationship can be such that the gay individual and the corporation can live comfortably with their differences–even with differences about certain deeply held beliefs and values regarding heterosexuality vs. homosexuality. As stated by a computer operations executive:

> It is regrettable that my boss, because of his strong devotion to Catholicism, cannot accept homosexuality as moral. The regrettable part is that he cannot share an opposite belief which is so important to me. However, we have worked out an agreement that he will support me as a competent professional and not undermine me publicly or privately. I, in turn, agreed to

never say or do anything, at work, which would make him feel that his religious beliefs about homosexuality were ridiculous. I guess we decided that we didn't need to convert each other. (Zoglin, 1979, p. 73)

The negotiation of this important difference supported each person's individuation in a way that both of them could live with, with relative ease. The gay individual could maintain his openness at work about being gay and maintain his integrity as a gay human being. Most important, in order to work out such an arrangement, each had not only to understand and value that the other was a different person, but also to recognize the particular manner in which the "different-ness" manifested itself. This is a high level dialogue between separate human beings, not just a form of interpersonal communication. Dialogue such as this represents a mode of empoweredness that is directed and purposeful. It is a type of self-actualization and manifestation that fosters the synergy of self and the situation. Actualization and Manifestation is where we must go.

Chapter 5, "On the Road," details the enablers:

• Introspection and Meditation;
• Creative Visualization and Active Imagination;
• Personal Responsibility and Autonomy; and
• Role Models and Support Groups.

It also elaborates on the specific action steps needed to reach the state of Actualization and Manifestation.

Chapter 5

On the Road

Not in his goals
but in his transitions
man is great.

– Ralph Waldo Emerson

Playing it safe is the most dangerous thing you can do. When safety is born, integrity dies. *If there is something to secure, secure integrity above all. In the end, it is all there is.*

The journey entails risk. Playing it safe comes from a deep-seated fear of abandonment and/or death. Therefore, fear is the central issue.

What then can you do? First, recognize that fear comes from a spiritual space, within which you do not know or refuse to accept and celebrate who you are–the wholeness and the integrity of being gay. Second, recognize that your adventure is the archetypical and heroic journey of Odysseus repeated. It is the inward travels and perils which test you by fate and within which you undertake the task of integrating divergent and fragmented parts into a whole. It is the great odyssey of integrity that leads to wholeness. *Unum.*

There is a starting point. There are risks. However, there are also enablers that foster and maintain the move toward empowerment. The starting point, much like the port for a ship, is the critical variable for success. The enablers will provide the support and nourishment necessary to continue the odyssey, regardless of the risk involved.

The point of departure is: homosexuality has nothing to do with choosing a life-style. It is not a choice! The concept of choice smacks of deciding between a gray flannel or blue pin-stripe suit. Homosexuality is a divine, magnificent gift–a legacy of creation. As with all gifts, it is to be appreciated with thankfulness and celebration. It is an endowment to be used to enrich yourself, your organization as a gay manager or executive, and the entire universe. This is the one and only starting point! It is the context within which integrity and wholeness provide Actualization and Manifestation, which are the goals of the odyssey.

Debris from earlier anti-gay experiences that still clutters your mind and spirit must be cleared out. The belief in the ontological goodness and purposefulness of homosexuality is prior to all else. It is the bulwark of the ship. Without it one *cannot* take the journey.

How do you acquire the belief and hold it diligently? First, you must experience, and thereby realize, the Reactive Wave: Self as a Result of the Situation. That is, you must have moved through the stages of Denial and Minimization, Retreat and Isolation, Anger and Conflict, and Depression and Victimization.

Second, you must feel OK about those growth experiences and be willing to begin the Internalization and Transformation process which permits the quantum leap from a discreetly negative and dependent energy state to a discreetly positive synergistic state. Thus, as in all things developmental, the starting point is paradoxical. It is a paradox because it is not a point in time or place. It occurs. And it occurs only after completing the Reactive Wave.

The enablers are the nourishment and support, the Dealing and Managing strategies, needed during the Proactive and Coactive Waves. These are the concrete enablers that permit and foster the move toward empowerment. They are:

- Introspection and Meditation;
- Creative Visualization and Active Imagination;
- Personal Responsibility and Autonomy; and
- Role Models and Support Groups.

While delineating the enablers, it is important to realize that Introspection is the transitional bridge between the Reactive and Proactive Waves. The transitional bridge, introspection, is built during the "ma" state addressed in Chapter 4. Diagram 5.1, The Transitional Bridge of Introspection, illustrates this concept. The transitional bridge is the "ma" state, the neutral zone, wherein you peel back that layer to accept and celebrate your homosexuality. It is the transitional, altered state wherein you begin to ask fundamental archetypal questions. "Is the journey worth the end?" "When I have stripped myself of my own homophobia will it have been worth the pain and effort?" This is where inner work takes place (Johnson, 1986). Inner work consists of meditation, creative visualization, and active imagination. These process enablers create the desired state of vision. The vision is the desired state of the Proactive Wave. Inner work, the stripping back of the conditioning layers, reveals the inner core of the person. Inner work causes the removal of the persona, thus exposing the inner core that is your integrity. Inner work requires meditation, creative visualization, and active imagination.

Meditation is a process of emptying yourself of what was. It is a process of cleaning, so as to rid the inner core of the layers of debris and junk that were placed there for safety during the Denial and Minimization Stage of the Reaction Wave. It is a process of cleaning, so as to empty and make room for Actualization and Manifestation. When you are in the state of Manifestation, you radiate the bright glow of integrity. You cannot radiate if you have not done your inner work.

Inner work, however, is not an end in itself. It is simply the neutral zone, the "ma" state, the transitional bridge between Victimization and Manifestation. It is not a place to get stuck in, which all too often happens. Later, I will discuss other enablers–Personal Responsibility and Autonomy, Role Models and Support Groups–which assure that you do not stay in the inner, interpersonal security state.

Creative visualization and active imagination will result in a desired state of vision and will create the strategies to achieve the vision. Once again, however, these processes require that you be empty of negative beliefs and values about your gayness. Inner work requires the removal of your own homophobia, and the excuses such as, "If it weren't for straights, etc."

Again the paradigm. The psyche does not like voids or vacuums. It will fill it up. Creative visualization, detailed earlier in Chapter 4,

DIAGRAM 5.1. The Transitional Bridge of Introspection

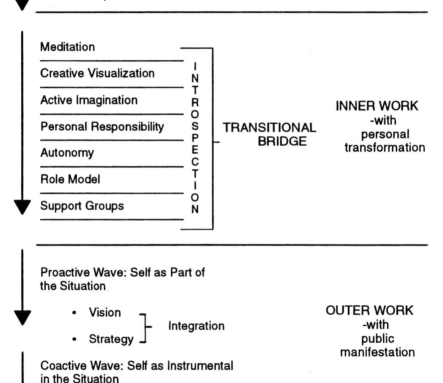

is the positive, active process of "filling up" the void with a desired state of vision.

Creative visualization is the mulling over, the reflecting upon, and the holding of a psychic vision of "what should be." Therefore, meditation and creative visualization provide the processes that will maximize awareness and cause the convergency of inner diversities and the rejection of the Reactive Wave as a place wherein you cannot experience your wholeness and integrity.

> Creative visualization is the technique of using your imagination to create what you want in your life. There is nothing at all new, strange, or unusual about creative visualization. You are already using it every day, every minute in fact. It is your natural power of imagination, the basic creative energy of the universe which you use constantly, whether or not you are aware of it.
>
> Imagination is the ability to create an idea or mental picture in your mind. In creative visualization you use your imagination to create a clear image of something you wish to manifest. Then you continue to focus on the idea of the picture regularly, giving it positive energy until it becomes objective reality . . . in other words, until you actually achieve what you have been visualizing. (Gawain, 1982, pp. 3-4)

We are back to our analogy of Moses. Unless you are able to see yourself as a "chosen person" you will continue to act as a slave.

As stated by a gay sales executive:

> You know, I could suddenly see myself as being more than okay. It was suddenly wonderful to be gay. The words "gay pride" now had meaning. It didn't necessarily mean marching in the streets, but what it did mean to me was that I went to work proud of who I was. I now move "gayly forward." (confidential interview)

Those who have accepted the risks associated with introspection and have found role models and support systems have developed the ability to make a mental shift. That shift is an image of yourself that no longer can operate under the wave of Reaction. Coping strategies are no longer enough. The step toward Actualization has been taken.

Active Imagination is a term and a process developed by Carl Gustav Jung. The process involves an active, inner dialogue between the unconscious and the conscious. It is sometimes likened to the process of dreaming, with the notable exception that you are fully alert and actively processing the dialogue (Johnson, 1986, p. 138).

Dr. Maria Von Franz (Unpublished lecture, Panoria Conference, Los Angeles, 1979) delineated the four phases of Active Imagination as:

- Empty the ego-mind;
- Let the unconscious flow into the vacuum;
- Add the ethical element; and
- Integrate the imagination back into the real, conscious world.

Robert Johnson (Johnson, 1986, p. 160) enumerated the above four phases as natural steps: (1) Invite the unconscious–the inner person states the dialogue; (2) Dialogue and experience–the willingness to listen to the unconscious and nonmanipulative reply with the conscious information, viewpoint, and values; (3) Add the ethical element of values–taking the ethical stand against primordial instinctual forces; and (4) Make it concrete with physical ritual–to make the abstract physical, rarify the abstract and connect it to one's physical, earthbound life.

Active Imagination is not widely known or "professionally" practiced outside Jungian circles. However, in this study, each of the 12 gay men of the 200 surveyed who live in the Coactive Wave, described using processes strikingly similar to Jung's process of Active Imagination.

What I describe as Meditation and Creative Visualization are steps one and two of Johnson's process. Steps three and four create the desired vision state (ethical element) and the strategies (internalization), which achieve the desired vision state of the Proactive Wave: Self as a Part of the Situation, which is an Internalization and Transformation State with the outcome of Synergy of the Self and the Situation.

Meditation, creative visualization, and active imagination are processes that create a vision. A vision is a desired state, a preferred future that you have come to while on the transitional bridge of introspection. The vision is a state of integrity that you can now put into words and you are willing to commit energy toward achieving and manifesting.

Meditation, creative visualization, and active imagination force you to take an internal, and eventually an external stand for a desired state of Actualization and Manifestation. These processes give you "a picture" of synergy before arriving at synergy. They also provide the infrastructure for the risk associated with the odyssey.

The desired state needs to be both spiritual and empirical. The desired state needs to be spiritual in order to keep the psyche focused on the possibilities of the "promised land" rather than falling back into the ruminations of the victim state. The spiritual aspects of wholeness, goodness, purposefulness, and integrity capture the psyche and thereby engage the spirit. Actualization and Manifestation is the radiation of integrity which emanated from vision held by the spirit. The concept equates to "the future is now." The Kahma Healers of Hawaii believe: Momawa–your moment of power is now; Ike–you create your own reality; Makia–you get what you concentrate on; and Kala–you are unlimited. Therefore, the future (the effect) is the cause of your present vision.

When your vision is a spiritual statement about your integrity, you proceed with purpose and direction. If it is not, you will retreat to the Reactive Wave.

Your vision is the gestalt expression of your integrity and therefore a radiation of who you are and a manifestation of what you want. If you do not have a vision, you are not in touch with your inner core and probably still view yourself as dependent on others for purpose and direction. Worse still, you will constantly be in a reactive mode when coping with your environment. In conclusion, your inability to state a vision and be committed to its achievement is the extent to which you are still in the Reactive Wave.

You know you have created a desired state of vision if it is:

- *Spiritual*, i.e., it is an (idealist) statement of the integrity, wholeness, goodness, and purposefulness of your homosexuality;

- *Individual*, i.e., it is a unique and personal statement that has come from your inner core;
- *Evolutionary*, i.e., it was developed through variations of the process of meditation, creative visualization, and active imagination; and
- *Synergistic*, i.e., it is a manifestation of your integrity that is totally satisfying, harmonious, and fulfills the highest good of all concerned.

Examples of visions could be:

- I am a divine, magnificent expression of power, love, life, and fulfillment. I celebrate, rejoice, and give thanks for the meaning, contribution, and service I offer the world and my corporation because I am uniquely gay and good.

-or-

- I am fulfilling my highest spiritual purpose as a gay executive. I am fulfilling the highest purpose of my corporation through my integrity and contribution. I love and approve of myself as a gay person and executive. Therefore, all that is left to do is to radiate who I am and thereby fulfill my purpose and achieve my vision.

If, in the beginning, you feel silly or embarrassed by such a visionary statement–good! That feeling is an indicator that you are on the right ship.

Earlier, I stated that visions need to be both spiritual and empirical. Having discussed the spiritual aspects, let me now detail the empirical dimensions. Empirical means capable of being observed and measured. Therefore, the vision requires concrete outcomes and strategies. Knowing about and acting upon the strategies is the second set of needed enablers.

One of the reasons for creating the vision during the "ma" state was to transit from the Reactive Wave to the Proactive Wave. The empirical dimension with its supportive strategies is the achievement of the Proactive Wave.

THE ACTION PLAN

At this point in the odyssey, you must become aware of, internalize, and implement a personal, individualized action plan. The following plan is one that I have used and validated during the research for this book. It is provided for illustrative purposes only. The reader must add, delete, and so forth, to make a plan. Diagram 5.2 illustrates the action plan.

Step 1: Communicate the Vision

Communicating your vision and modeling your vision, which comes first? This question is much like the ancient philosophical chicken and egg debate. For purposes of symmetry, I will begin with the "expression" of the vision as the first "proactive" step.

In the Proactive Wave, it behooves you to verbalize your vision to your corporation. Not an easy task, but an accomplishable one. This communication is not to be confused with "coming out of the closet." That event occurred during the Reactive Wave. What I am stating here is that how you choose to verbalize your ontological goodness as a gay manager or executive, in terms of your contribution and service to the corporation, is the most crucial variable of all the strategies.

Communicating the vision is selling. Selling entails:

- causation verbiage;
- identifying buyer benefits;
- a selling style; and
- a power base.

Selling the vision entails what Martin Seligman calls "causation" themes (Seligman, 1989) which inspire confidence and influence the receiver of the message to buy the concept. Optimistic, action-oriented-words such as: "I will; I am going to; We shall; and Let us" convince the receiver that you have internalized your vision and you are willing to commit yourself to its achievement. Whereas, pessimistic, duty-oriented words such as: "I must; I will have to; We should; and We ought to" do not convince the receiver of any commitment beyond duty. The point here is–how often have you

DIAGRAM 5.2. The Coactive Wave Action Plan

STEP 1: COMMUNICATE THE VISION

- Causation verbiage
- Identify buyer benefits
- Selling style
- Power Base
    - Push style: Authoritative
    - Pull style: Collaborative

STEP 2: MODEL A STANDARD OF BEHAVIOR THAT RADIATES THE VISION

- Do   – Collaborative conflict resolution
    - Know the opponent's position better than the opponent and respond appropriately
    - Maintain the highest standard of business achievement and ethical behavior
    - Maintain the highest level of supervisory and managerial knowledge and skill
- Do Not   – Degrade other gays, but do not defend other gays simply because they are gay
    - Presume to speak for all gays
    - Be apologetic or defensive about homosexuality

STEP 3: TAKE PERSONAL RESPONSIBILITY FOR ACHIEVING THE VISION

- Purposeful and meaningful activities
- Contribution and service
- Integrity
- Positive impact on others

STEP 4: IDENTIFY AND UTILIZE GAY ROLE MODELS AND SUPPORT GROUPS

- Role models as "wayshowers"
- Support groups as mutual aid groups

fallen into the trap of defending your contribution and service to your corporation? You need to communicate, with optimistic, action-oriented words, the unique meaning, contribution, and service you provide to the corporation. Such an expression illustrates to the receiver/buyer of your vision the values and what you will contribute, not what you hope to contribute!

Second, selling the vision requires identifying the benefits of the vision to others, i.e., what is in it for them? All too frequently, one sells the features and does not close the sale. For example, my car has a hole in its roof. I did not buy "a hole in the roof," I bought a "sun roof." Again, one does not buy the particulars of a fuel injection system, but rather one is buying the benefit of fuel economy.

What does this have to do with communicating your vision? Well, answer this: What is in it for your corporation to have you whole and complete? How does your integrity affect your contribution and service to your corporation? How does your vision contribute to your corporation being useful and successful? How does your vision translate into a positive impact upon your colleagues? In this day of teamwork, what in your vision makes you a good team builder and/or team player? How does your vision help your associates, and thereby the corporation, to become more open, risk-taking, innovative, and thus more competitive? The answer to these types of questions is: the buyer (corporation) benefits. You take the benefits and create the causation verbiage with which to communicate your vision.

In the restaurant business, the presentation of the dish (the benefits and causation verbiage) and the service (the delivery) make or break the restaurant regardless of the preparation of the food (the vision). Communicating the vision now entails the delivery, that is, a selling style. The selling includes various power-based styles of delivery from which to choose.

Selling styles can be simplistically described and categorized as a "push" style or a "pull" style. A push style is usually very persuasive and logically convincing using words such as "you should, you must, and you ought to . . . "–pessimistic, duty-oriented words. It is usually presented in a rational, logical approach which focuses on the features rather than the benefits. Remember the time you bought the shirt and tie you really did not want, because you just wanted to get away from the salesperson? Well, the salesperson was probably using a "push" selling style. The push style usually results in one-time sales, no repeat business from the buyer, or no sale at all.

A pull style, however, is usually very participatory, involving a discussion with the buyer. Words such as: "Were you looking for this or that . . . How do you plan to use this? Let's consider this approach . . ." (optimistic, action-oriented words), are examples of the directional, purposeful, yet facilitatory "pull" style. The pull style uses a valuing approach which permits the buyer to do comparison-selection from options and thereby get the appropriate item with more value for the expenditure. Remember the time you were ready to buy all the whistles and bells that only come with the flashy, but ineffective, stereo system? However, the salesperson directed you to a more user-friendly system. Well, the salesperson probably used a "pull" sales style. The pull selling style results in a satisfied buyer with whom the seller has developed a harmonious relationship. The buyer trusts the seller and will return.

The point here is: The selling style with which you choose to communicate your vision has a great deal to do with whether or not you achieve integration into your corporation. Bear in mind, assimilation means "let's all be alike," whereas integration means "let's respect diversity." The integration of yourself into the corporation is the desired outcome of the Proactive Wave.

The push style has an authoritative power base. Diagram 5.3 illustrates this concept. Bear in mind Carse's work (1986) discussed earlier in Chapter 3. The Authoritative power base is a finite game. If you choose to persuade, convince, confront, etc., you are still in the Reactive Wave–believing and acting as if you are the result of your situation rather than in control of your situation.

The pull style has a collaborative power base. Diagram 5.4 illustrates this concept. The collaborative power base is the infinite game described by Carse (1986). If you choose to participate, discuss, and value the other person while holding firm to your vision, then you are in the Coactive Wave–believing and acting as an integrated, not assimilated individual.

The simple point I have been trying to make is: "You get more flies with a spoonful of honey than with all the vinegar in the

DIAGRAM 5.3. Authoritative Power Base of the Push Style

<u>Seller</u>	<u>Buyer</u>
Coercive Power	Must be FEARFUL
Information Power	Must have less DATA
Expert Power	Must have less EXPERIENCE
Role Power	Must have a lesser TITLE
Reward Power and Punishment	Must have a <u>need</u>, not a
	want, for the GOODS,
	SERVICES, or MONEY

world!'' Diagram 5.5, illustrates the entire process of communicating your vision.

Step 2: Model a Standard of Behavior that Radiates the Vision

The second step in the action plan is to model an ethical stand and behave in a manner that is congruent with your integrity. During this step one must be aware of, concentrate on, and consciously practice the following "Do's and Don'ts" (Olson, 1986, pp. 8-11).

- Do start with a collaborative conflict resolution model;
- Do know any opponent's position better than the opponent;
- Do maintain the highest standard of business achievement and ethical behavior;
- Do maintain the highest level of supervisory management knowledge and skill;
- Do not degrade other gays, but do not defend other gays simply because they are gay;
- Do not presume to speak for all gays; and
- Do not be apologetic or defensive about homosexuality.

DIAGRAM 5.4. Collaborative Power Base for the Pull Style

<u>Seller</u>	<u>Buyer</u>
Has integrity	Knows the seller can be trusted
Is egalitarian	Feels valued as an intelligent human being
Uses referent power	Gives the seller control and power
	Enables and empowers the seller

Do Start with a Collaborative Conflict Resolution Model

Collaborating is a style of conflict resolution. It is based on the assumption that both parties in the disagreement have the possibility of "getting what they want." It is both assertive and cooperative, that is, "I want what is right for me and what is right for you." It is a style that believes in "win-win" resolution. Collaborating involves an attempt to work with the other person to find some solution which fully satisfies the concerns of both persons. It means digging into an issue to identify the underlying concerns of the two individuals and finding an alternative that meets both sets of concerns. Collaborating between two persons might take the form of exploring a disagreement to learn from each other's insight, concluding to resolve some condition which would otherwise have them competing for resources, or confronting and trying to find a creative solution to an interpersonal problem (Blake and Mouton, 1970).

The caveat to this style is that each party must be a reasonable human being and be willing to explore the possible resolution that is fully satisfying to all concerned. If this is not the case, this does not then mean that you should move to the confrontational style of Reactive Wave, this is, "I get 100 and you get nothing!" However, what it does mean is that the collaborating style is a beginning point and establishes you as one having integrity. It also permits movement to other styles such as avoiding and/or compromising before

DIAGRAM 5.5. Communicating Your Vision of an Integrated, Service-Based, Contributing Gay Manager

<u>Reactive</u>
- Rumination verbiage – inspires concern and threatens the other

<u>Proactive</u>
- Causation verbiage – inspires confidence and influences the other

<u>Seller Benefits</u>
- What are the features described by the gay manager?

<u>Buyer Benefits</u>
- What is in it for the corporation?

<u>Authoritative Power</u>
- Coercive
- Information
- Expert
- Role
- Reward and punishment

F
I
N
I
T
E

<u>Collaborative Power</u>
- Integrity
- Egalitarian
- Referent

I
N
F
I
N
I
T
E

<u>Push Selling Style</u>
- Rational Approach
  - persuasive
  - convincing

<u>Pull Selling Style</u>
- Valuing Approach
  - participation
  - discussion

<u>Outcome</u>
- One-time sale or no sale with short-term commitment
- "Victimized"–assimilated gay manager

<u>Outcome</u>
- Sale with long-term commitment
- Empowered, enabled–integrated gay manager

arriving at confrontation, thus giving you many more options to resolve differences and maintain your integrity.

Collaboration only occurs if one has done the inner work addressed earlier. There is an intrinsic sense of worth (integrity) that comes as a result of effective interdependent, collaborative conflict resolution. There is wholeness in knowing that win/win does indeed exist and that work life does not have to be any form of lose/win, that there are almost always harmonious resolutions that provide the highest good for all concerned.

Do Know the Opponent's Position Better than the Opponent and Respond Appropriately

One is paranoid if he believes that 100 percent of his corporation is after him because he is gay. However, one is not paranoid if he realizes and prepares himself for the 1 to 2 percent of the corporation who are probably homophobic.

> Very few homophobes read our literature. They will not come to us to refute the fine points of our movement. They will come instead armed with a few–and they are very few–stock positions, all of which have to do with the notion that homosexuality is sinful, sick, and/or criminal . . . . But, their arguments, as near as I can tell, continue to be the same simplistic, prejudicial, uninformed drivel that has passed from generation to generation. (Olson, 1986, p. 10)

The point Olson is making is that the content of the homophobic viewpoint is simple and therefore easily refuted by intelligence, insight, and facts. However, when responding to homophobic arguments it is vital to maintain inner composure. Do not take their bait and respond with anger exhibited by shouting, etc. Do not imitate their behavior; that is their finite game. If you play their game, they win. Rather, start with your inner belief that you are the one with the "good news" of the integrity of your homosexuality. Your inner belief will help you to respond in a nondefensive, but firm, even-toned affirmative voice.

Earlier, I stated that collaboration requires both task maturity (knowing what one is talking about) and relationship maturity (ability to listen and discuss). Homophobes have neither. Give up the need to discuss the issues with them; that only empowers them and disempowers you. Give up the need to convert them to your point of view. Homophobes are "people of the lies," and they have chosen to block themselves into the Anger and Conflict stage. A firm, nondefensive, hit-and-run, broken record, even-toned, gay-affirming response is more effective. Even more important, such a response empowers you and maintains your goal of modeling a standard of behavior that radiates your vision.

Do Maintain the Highest Standard of Business Achievement and Ethical Behavior

As detailed in Chapter 1, competency does not guarantee acceptance, promotions, etc. However, it is a necessary foundation. The gay manager or executive does have to do better than his straight counterparts. Right now, that's the way it is. To believe and act otherwise is dangerous. To change the double standard, regretfully, means that one has to maintain the highest standards of business achievement so as not to give the opposition any room for debate. To do these one must, first, behave as if the business were his own. One does not want hidden agendas and undermining politics to take place in his business. You would want your employees engaged in tasks that have purpose and value. Modeling such behavior radiates your vision, has a positive effect on others, and empowers you.

Next, one must establish and maintain the highest possible standard of ethical behavior. Why? First of all, ethical behavior should be the given. Second, 83 percent of those interviewed cited examples wherein corporate leaders tried to nail them on an ethical technicality when their competency was impeccable.

I subcontracted and served on the advisory board of a management consulting firm which dismissed a gay colleague for an ethical breach. The gay consultant held a PhD and had the second highest evaluations from training classes in the corporation. His efforts resulted in repeat business; his client service was flawless. However, he was too overtly gay for the office manager and the president of the corporation. In my opinion, the office manager watched the gay consultant like a hawk. The office manager discerned that the gay consultant had been charging the company taxi fare to and from the airport, but in reality the gay consultant's lover had been transporting him. This breach in ethics was all that was needed. My hands were tied. As a board member I could not defend his behavior. However, I was the only board member who felt that the gentleman should be reprimanded but not dismissed. All remaining board members, hardly ethical saints themselves, insisted on dismissal. Another interesting twist to this story is that one of the board members, whose business is diversity training, was one of the most vehement for dismissal. The president, office manager, and diversity trainer were also all personal and long-time friends. I am sure, to this day, they would deny that the real reason the consultant was dismissed was that he was too overtly gay. Even in the most liberal of organizations, homophobia can rear its ugly head, look around, and stalk gay individuals until it finds something. As in the case above, ethics, if competency is present, will be the focus for dismissal.

This is not to set up a no-win situation that would require spotless behavior. It is simply to say one should behave ethically anyway. Therefore, there will be nothing to be concerned about.

What are ethics? Ethical behavior is based on a moral viewpoint which has its roots in our value system which is housed in our integrity. Homosexual integrity states: "Homosexuality is a divine, magnificent gift to be appreciated with thankfulness and celebration." I have dealt at length earlier with the concept of integrity as the foundation of ethical behavior.

Values, morals, and ethics, however, are distinct, although related, concepts. They can be briefly defined as follows:

> *Values:* our personally prized beliefs, i.e., individual *beliefs* which underpin moral judgment as well as ultimately supporting ethical systems;
> *Morals:* the sense of right and wrong—our morals are *judgments* we make; and
> *Ethics:* a framework developed to help guide, influence, and determine our *behaviors* in response to specific situations—how we choose what we *do* to demonstrate our values and moral stands.

DIAGRAM 5.6. The Building Blocks of Ethical Behavior

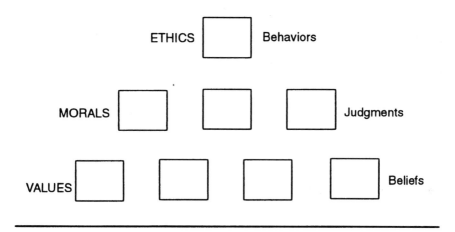

Diagram 5.6 illustrates the relationship of values, morals, and ethics. Values are the beliefs which we prize and are likely to publicly affirm when appropriate. Values serve as the underpinnings for both our moral standards and our ethical systems. They are chosen freely and are personally and strongly held. Some examples of values might be: "I believe in the sanctity of homosexuality" or, "I believe that all gays should always act with integrity and honesty."

Values can arise from a wide variety of sources. Family, friends, schooling, religion, the media, etc., can each–or all–strongly influence the values we choose to embrace. While our values can (and often do) change with time and experience, they tend to change rather slowly, and only when faced with potent evidence that our currently held values are no longer viable or tenable. This shift for most gays occurred during the Internalization and Transformation Stage. Values, then, are the very basic elements that help determine both our moral codes and our ethical systems.

Morals are the judgments we make concerning our own and/or others' values and actions. They tend to be "black and white" and to be couched in terms of right or wrong. Our moral standards are based on *our own* values but may be strongly influenced by the moral standards generally held by one's subculture. I believe that all gays should always act with integrity and honesty (value), therefore any form of discrimination is wrong (moral).

We apply moral judgments to both values and ethical systems (behaviors). We often use moral judgments to help us determine both the "correctness" of values and the "rightness" of actions. They serve as an "auditing" function which helps us determine if our beliefs are consistent with our behaviors.

Andy Warhol once said, "Art is what you can get away with." Today, we seem to apply that philosophy to morals and ethics. What we need to keep our eye on is the prize of integrity, which requires that we protect integrity above all, for in the end it is all we have.

We develop an ethical framework and use it to help guide, influence, and ultimately determine or choose our actions in regard to a given situation. Our ethics are based upon our values; given those values, ethical systems enable us to make decisions about how to act, especially when the situation at hand is ambiguous or falls into a "gray area." There are any number of ethical frameworks which we select to use because they are "workable." That is, they result in decisions and behaviors that are consistent with the values we profess. Diagram 5.7 illustrates the above concept.

Finally, then, one develops an ethical framework (including principles and guidelines) that guides or influences one's choice of action(s) in those situations where harm or benefit to others is involved. Ethical decisions do not involve "pat" answers, require careful examination of the facts of the given situation, and oblige us to look beyond our own self-interests to consider the effects of our proposed actions on the well-being of others and of society-at-large.

Kohlberg's model is the most frequently cited model of ethical development (Kohlberg, 1969). The model is based on the notion that stages of ethical development occur in an invariable sequence with each stage arising from the previous one and being more cognitively and spiritually complex than its predecessor. Kohlberg's research methodology was similar to that employed in the surveys of this book. His methodology involved assessing levels of ethical development by presenting subjects with a series of ethical dilemmas and asking them for an evaluation of the ethical conflict. Kohlberg's model is summarized in Diagram 5.8.

DIAGRAM 5.7. Building and Maintaining Ethical Behavior

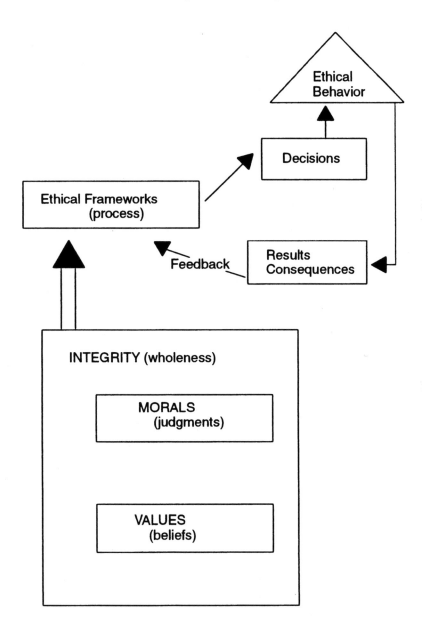

DIAGRAM 5.8. Kohlberg's Stages of Ethical Development

LEVEL 1:   **Preconventional Ethics**
(Ages 4-10)
Stage 1: Punishment-Obedience Orientation
Moral judgment based on a desire to avoid <u>punishment</u>.
Stage 2: Instrumental-Relativist Orientation
Individual is motivated by a desire to satisfy own needs.

LEVEL 2:   **Conventional Ethics**
(Ages 10-13)
Stage 3: "Good Boy/Nice Girl" Orientation
Individual motivated by a desire to avoid disapproval or dislike of others.
Stage 4: Law and Order Orientation
Moral judgments based on a desire to avoid censure by a legitimate authority.

LEVEL 3:   **Postconventional Ethics**
(Adolescence to Adulthood; not reached by most adults)
Stage 5: Legalistic Orientation
Individual concerned with maintaining the respect of equals and the community, maintaining social order, and obeying democratically determined laws.
Stage 6: Universal Ethical Principles Orientation
Individual's own conscience is the only criterion of values, morals, and ethical conduct.

Although Kohlberg places his levels within age ranges, it is clear that many so-called adults do not reach Postconventional Ethics. This developmental concept is similar to the corelational discussion in Chapter 4 regarding the relationship of:

- Adulthood–Interdependence–Empowerment
- Adolescence–Independence–Disempowerment
- Childhood–Dependence–Disempowerment

Diagram 5.9 illustrates the linkage between Kolhberg's Stages of Ethical Development and the Gay Model of Transition.

If individuals are on a development track they are progressing from Childhood to Adulthood, from disempowerment to empowerment, from the Conventional ethics to Postconventional ethics and moving from the Reactive Wave to the Coactive Wave in the Gay Model of Transition.

We have been discussing ethics because to establish and maintain the highest possible standard of ethical behavior places one beyond business reproach, thus empowering and enabling one to function in a coactive manner in the workplace.

Do Maintain the Highest Level of Supervisory and Managerial Knowledge and Skill

Covey tells the following insightful story:

> Suppose you were to come upon someone in the woods working feverishly to saw down a tree.
>
> "What are you doing?" you ask.
>
> "Can't you see?" comes the impatient reply. "I'm sawing down this tree."
>
> "You look exhausted!" you exclaim. "How long have you been at it?"
>
> "Over five hours," he returns, "and I'm beat! This is hard work."
>
> "Well, why don't you take a break for a few minutes and sharpen that saw?" you inquire. "I'm sure it would go a lot faster."
>
> "I don't have time to sharpen the saw," the man says emphatically. "I'm too busy sawing!" (Covey, 1989, p. 287)

"Sharpen the saw" training and development is crucial to any activity or career. Gay managers and executives, like their heterosexual counterparts in corporate America, were most probably promoted because of their technical expertise (the task side) and not necessarily for their managerial ability (the human side). All too frequently, the human side is considered as a secondary, "natural" occurrence. As we move into the complexity of the year 2000, however, many corporations are discovering that to ignore good management and leadership development is to watch the corporation muck around in quicksand.

DIAGRAM 5.9. Kohlberg's Stages of Ethical Development and the Gay Model of Transition

GAY MODEL OF TRANSITION				KOHLBERG'S STAGES OF ETHICAL DEVELOPMENT
STAGE	**WAVE**	**STRATEGY**	**OUTCOME**	
I. Denial and Minimization	REACTIVE Self as a result of the situation	C O P I N G	Situationally Dependent	**LEVEL 1:** **Preconventional Ethics** (Ages 4-10) Stage 1: Punishment-Obedience Orientation Moral judgment based on a desire to avoid punishment Stage 2: Instrumental-Relativist Orientation Individuals motivated by a desire to satisfy own needs.
II. Retreat and Isolation				
III. Anger and Conflict				
IV. Depression and Victimization				
V. Internalization and Transformation	PROACTIVE Self as a part of the situation	D E A L I N G	Integration of Self in Situation	**LEVEL 2:** **Conventional Ethics** (Ages 10-13) Stage 3: "Good Boy/Nice Girl" Orientation Individual motivated by a desire to avoid disapproval or dislike of others. Stage 4: Law and Order Orientation Moral judgments based on a desire to avoid censure by a legitimate authority.
VI. Actualization and Manifestation	COACTIVE Self as instrumental in the situation	M A N A G I N G	Synergy of Self and Situation	**LEVEL 3:** **Postconventional Ethics** (Adolescence to Adulthood; not reached by most adults) Stage 5: Legalistic Orientation Individual concerned with maintaining the respect of equals and the community, maintaining social order, and obeying democratically determined laws. Stage 6: Universal Ethical Principles Orientation Individual's own conscience is the only criterion of values, morals, and ethical conduct.

A heterosexual manager can rely longer on his technical expertise and downplay his managerial expertise, as long as he delivers the bottom line and fits the corporate paradigm of competency, i.e., white, male, married, etc., as discussed in Chapter 2. He has the "privileged paradigm" to fall back on.

My company specializes in management training and development, therefore, I have a deep belief in the necessity of sharpening the managerial saw for everyone. It is even more important for the gay manager and/or executive. First, because it is the ethical/right thing to do. One owes it to one's associates who expect to be managed and lead in an effective and affective manner. Second, as found in the survey and interviews undertaken in this effort, case after case was cited regarding gay individuals who were demoted from managerial positions more frequently than their heterosexual counterparts. The reason (more likely the excuse) was the lack of management and leadership skills. Diagram 5.10 illustrates key managerial and leadership knowledge and skill areas for development. Sharpen your managerial saw!

Do Not Degrade Other Gays, but Do Not Defend Other Gays Simply Because They Are Gay

You and other gays have had enough negative experiences. It is unacceptable behavior to talk about or gossip about your fellow gays. To do so discloses to the corporation that you have not dealt with your own homophobia and provides gunpowder for the enemy. It is acceptable and appropriate behavior to debate and disagree with fellow gays as one would with anyone. Corporations need difference of opinion in order to select the most creative and effective product or service. It is generally poor policy to put down anyone. If you get a reputation for degrading others and especially other gays, your integrity is questioned by everyone. No one trusts a degrader, nor sees such behavior as a sign of strength!

We all are probably very aware of the damage done by blatant degradation. However, anyone can be guilty of subtle degradation. For example, *The Washington Post* carried a picture of a person in drag after DC's Gay Pride Day. One gay executive I know said: "Isn't it just like that? It happens every time. The *Post* reinforced

DIAGRAM 5.10. Managerial and Executive Development: Credibility, Sensitivity, and Competency

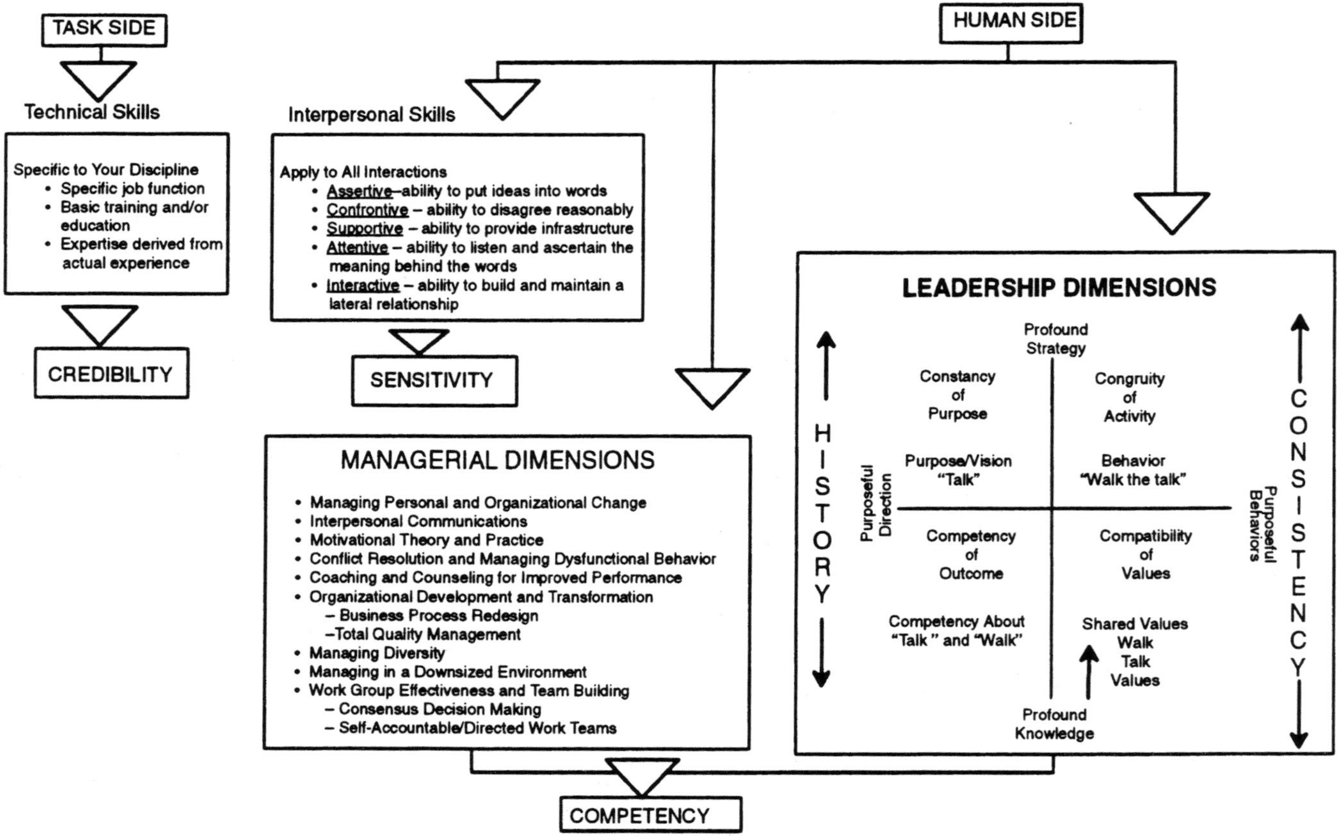

TASK SIDE

Technical Skills

Specific to Your Discipline
- Specific job function
- Basic training and/or education
- Expertise derived from actual experience

CREDIBILITY

HUMAN SIDE

Interpersonal Skills

Apply to All Interactions
- **Assertive** – ability to put ideas into words
- **Confrontive** – ability to disagree reasonably
- **Supportive** – ability to provide infrastructure
- **Attentive** – ability to listen and ascertain the meaning behind the words
- **Interactive** – ability to build and maintain a lateral relationship

SENSITIVITY

MANAGERIAL DIMENSIONS

- Managing Personal and Organizational Change
- Interpersonal Communications
- Motivational Theory and Practice
- Conflict Resolution and Managing Dysfunctional Behavior
- Coaching and Counseling for Improved Performance
- Organizational Development and Transformation
  – Business Process Redesign
  – Total Quality Management
- Managing Diversity
- Managing in a Downsized Environment
- Work Group Effectiveness and Team Building
  – Consensus Decision Making
  – Self-Accountable/Directed Work Teams

COMPETENCY

LEADERSHIP DIMENSIONS

CONSISTENCY

HISTORY

Purposeful Behaviors

Purposeful Direction

Profound Strategy

Profound Knowledge

Constancy of Purpose
Purpose/Vision "Talk"

Congruity of Activity
Behavior "Walk the talk"

Competency of Outcome

Compatibility of Values

Competency About "Talk" and "Walk"

Shared Values
Walk
Talk
Values

102

the stereotypes. Now the public will be even more convinced that we are all a bunch of screaming queens."

His intent is not in question. Yes, the *Post* photographer most probably went out of his/her way to get such a photo. Furthermore, the photo probably sold papers. The gay executive's outcome is in question! If he is still at a point of giving his power over to the concerns of "what will the straight community think," he has not empowered himself. Does he think that when a straight person reads about a heterosexual child abuse case s/he says, "What will the gay community think?" Of course not, and how absurd! I am in no way equating drag with heterosexual child abuse. I am using the extreme of child abuse to make the point. Let us celebrate all the diversity within our community and let us not disempower ourselves by giving our power away, through being concerned about what the majority will think.

Sometimes we give our power over to the heterosexual community because we want to conform. Conformity leaves little room for celebrating all the diversity of our community: drag, leather, western, "gray flannel suit," etc. Marianne Williamson, in her profound work *A Return to Love*, states:

We can't fake authenticity. We think we need to create ourselves, always doing a paste-up job on our personalities. That is because we're trying to be special rather than real. We're pathetically trying to conform with all the other people trying to do the same.

A tulip doesn't strive to impress anyone. It doesn't struggle to be different than a rose. It doesn't have to. It *is* different. And there's room in the garden for every flower. You didn't have to struggle to make your face different than anyone else's on earth. It just is. You *are* unique because you were created that way. Look at little children in kindergarten. They're all different without trying to be. As long as they're unselfconsciously being themselves, they can't help but shine. It's only later, when children are taught to compete, to strive to be better than others, that their natural light becomes distorted. (Williamson, 1992, p. 163)

Yet, when one thinks and acts as the gay executive in question, one is not celebrating and rejoicing in the diversity of what it means to be gay. Simply put, do not degrade any gay for his appropriate ethical choices and expressions. To do so degrades yourself and the gay community and empowers the opposition. Recall in Chapter 1, I addressed the Conversion and Dominance Dynamic of corporations. One disempowering strategy is to try to think, look, and act like the majority and to avoid identification with outward expressions of gayness.

On the other hand, it is just as disempowering to defend other gays simply because they are gay. If a fellow gay business colleague has done something that violates the corporation's business ethics, you should not defend that behavior with excuses. He behaved unethically and must assume responsibility for his behavior. Unethical behavior is unethical behavior regardless of the performer. To approve of his behavior is disempowering for you and all concerned. Furthermore to do so violates your integrity.

Do Not Presume to Speak for All Gays

A pitfall often experienced by any minority is to be placed in the position of speaking for his/her entire minority group. This strategy is an attempt by the majority to make the minority defensive. Get ready when you hear, "Well, how do homosexuals feel about . . . ?" You cannot speak for all gays. We are as diverse, and have the right to be as diverse, as the straight community. A tall, thin, straight, white male does not get asked such broad questions and therefore does not fall into the trap of defending all straight behavior. To speak for all gays is individually disempowering. To collaboratively discuss your particular issue with your particular viewpoint will empower you and assist you to maintain your integrity.

Do Not Be Apologetic or Defensive About Homosexuality

This rule comes as a final point, because if you have done all of the above you are not apologetic about your gift of homosexuality.

No argument is more persuasive than the life nobly lived.

The best defense remains a superb offense, one that celebrates your identity and that offers itself as a gift by which the rest of the world can be enriched. (Olson, 1986, p. 11)

In summary, the above "Do's and Don'ts" are strategies that help achieve Step 2 of the Proactive Wave Action Plan. That is, modeling a standard of behavior that radiates one's vision.

Step 3: Take Personal Responsibility for Achieving the Vision

Personal responsibility is the key. Taking personal responsibility means facing the consequences of our actions. If you choose to stay in the closet, then you have to be ready to face the consequences and accept all the pain of the decay of your integrity. In the corporate world, this is manifested through all the manipulation that closeted gays use to covertly influence others, i.e., the counterfeiting and closet maintenance addressed in Chapter 4. However, if you wish to take the odyssey to integrity then you have to be ready to face the consequences of the pain of enlightenment. If you wish to do away with pain, that is not an option!

Taking personal responsibility means becoming self-accountable. Self-accountable gay managers characteristically:

- Value and celebrate their gayness as a precious gift;
- Value and understand their contributions to their corporation;
- Value the corporation's contribution to them.

Taking personal responsibility consists of empowering and enabling ourselves through individuation to achieve our vision. Although empowerment was defined and discussed in Chapter 4, it is important to review it here in regard to taking personal responsibility.

Empowerment means claiming and radiating our personal power-integrity through activating what Block calls "Enlightened Self-Interest" (Block, 1986, pp. 79-84). Block describes enlightened self-interest as follows:

- *Meaning.* We decide that we will engage in activities that have meaning to us and are genuinely needed, even if we think they may not win approval or blessings from those around us. We commit to the pursuit of substance.

- *Contribution and Service.* We decide to do things that we feel genuinely contribute to the organization and its purpose.
- *Integrity.* To maintain our integrity in organizations is essential to be people of the truth.
- *Positive Impact on Others.* It is in everyone's self-interest to treat others well. All of us must care deeply about the well-being of our colleagues and the people around us.

Empowerment is based on the personal choices we make that are expressed by our own enlightened self-interest actions. To express or radiate our enlightened self-interest is to:

- Act in a manner that exhibits that power is in our own hands, i.e., the Do's and Don'ts detailed above;
- Act upon the underlying purpose of our vision, i.e., Steps 1 and 2 of the Proactive Wave Action Plan, and;
- Commit ourselves, body and soul, to achieving the vision now, i.e., creating conditions under which you as well as others do not have to violate integrity in order to thrive in your corporation.

Thus empowerment comes from acting on our own enlightened self-interest.

Empowering ourselves enables us. Enabling is a process of removing real, actual barriers to our self-actualization as gay managers. Removing barriers is achieved through what Carl Jung termed individuation. Jung wrote, "I use the term 'individuation' to denote the process by which a person becomes a psychological 'individual,' that is, a separate, indivisible unity of 'whole'" (Jung, 1971, Vol. 9i, p. 275).

A person who remains oblivious of himself and of the world around him cannot be a very individuated person. He must, therefore, also be integrated. Individuation and integration go hand in hand, so that differentiation and psychological unification are coexisting processes.

Individuation is the decision to act out of our own power center–integrity of being gay. We accept responsibility to create a future of our own choosing–the actualization of our vision as a coactive, whole gay individual who is integrated, not assimilated, in his corporate world. The outcome for individuation is that we live our own life and have control over our own destiny.

The alternative, which is the victim's choice, is to act out someone else's vision. To do so is to be a willing victim. Willing victims are people of the lie, acting out someone else's choices and thereby not responsible or holding themselves accountable. Taking personal responsibility for our vision is our essential act of integrity.

Step 4: Identify and Utilize Gay Role Models and Support Systems

Role models and support systems are the fourth enabling factor. Situational grouping, mutual aid groups–congregating with people who are experiencing similar discontinuities to work on the problems and opportunities presented by the transition–was a key element in Adam, Hayes, and Hapson's (1976) study regarding coping tasks in transitional events.·

> Support systems–this concept has been most clearly developed by Seashore (1974) who makes the use of appropriate support systems his key aid to coping with transitional stress. He points out to clients that the effective use of support systems can lead from social isolation to social integration; from vulnerability to assistance; from emotional isolation to intimacy; from feelings of powerlessness to feelings of self-worth; from stimulus isolation (in a rut) to broadened perspectives; from environmental isolation to access to resources. (p. 17)

In this study those who had support groups such as local affiliates of the National Association of Business Councils, a gay and lesbian business association, AT&T's League, and others, reported that movement away from the "victimization" feeling was facilitated by members of their support group. As stated by a gay personnel director:

> If it hadn't been for GGBC (Golden Gate Business Council, San Francisco, CA), I do not know how I would have gotten through this mess. Just having someone to talk to about all the absurdities really helped. There was this one guy, who had

been through similar problems, who helped me understand how I was setting myself up for the kill. It really gave me a lot to think about. (confidential interview)

Twenty-six years ago, in 1969, the New York Metropolitan Police Department went on a "fag-bashing" raid of New York City gay bars. Much to their surprise, when they arrived at the Stonewall bar, the "queens" fought back to the point of smashing police car windshields with parking meters ripped from the ground. After Stonewall, there was no turning back. Over the past 26 years, leaders and role models have emerged. The September 8, 1975, *Time* magazine cover featured Sgt. Leonard Matlovich with the phrase, "I Am a Homosexual." In 1980, *The Washingtonian* cover featured Mayor Marion Barry standing between a gay leader and a lesbian leader. The caption read, "Is DC Becoming the Gay Capital of America?" In 1985, *The Life and Times of Harvey Milk* won an Oscar for the best documentary film. Role models show us the way. They point the way. They are "wayshowers." Their lives tell us it can be done.

Everywhere one turns, there are now archetypes such as Senator Studds, Congressman Frank, and Bruce Lehman, Assistant Commerce Secretary. These models, examples of those who have survived—no, more than survived, they have thrived on being who they are and have successfully integrated themselves into the weave of society—are serving as blueprints for gays who wish to make the transition from disempowerment to empowerment.

As noted previously, the American corporate world lags behind society at large. There are gay executives, but very few of them are out of the closet enough to be visible to the general public. However, archetypes are beginning to develop.

_____ always seems to have his wits about him. He always seems to just calmly and assertively move forward. Everyone knew he was gay, but he never seemed to take "the bait." When he became VP of Operations, we all knew we could do it too! (confidential interview)

THE RISKS OF THE ODYSSEY

The theme of this chapter has been that if there is something to secure, secure integrity above all. In the end, it is all there is.

To take any journey involves risk. My work as an organizational psychologist requires a great deal of travel. Thousands of air miles with hundreds of cabs entails danger. However, if I were to focus on the risks and not the purposefulness and outcome of my work, I probably would not travel! Remember our discussion of "existential suffering" in Chapter 4? So it is with the odyssey from disempowerment to empowerment. Therefore, I have left the discussion of the risks until the end of this chapter. I hope I have shown in Chapters 1 through 4, that the outcome of the odyssey is well worth the risks associated with it.

From my personal experience, the outcome of the odyssey–empowerment–is well worth the discrimination, homophobia, job loss, etc., that I have experienced along the way.

I hesitate to tell horror stories about being gay because it requires revisiting the Reactive Wave. However, story-telling–the sharing of experiences–may indeed help others to know that the journey to empowerment is possible.

I entered a Catholic seminary at a very young age. I spent my teenage formative years and my twenties as a monk. At one point, I discovered that I was attracted to another Brother. I prayed and avoided. Once, as fate would have it, we ended up alone together in an office, working on a research project. He hugged me, kissed me, and held me. That was it! Being a pious, scrupulous sort, guilt took over. I went to confession.

Now the real story begins. The seal of confession was blatantly broken. The priest told my superior. The superior called me and the other monk to his office. My breath was taken away! I was told that "The seal of confession does not apply to this mortal situation." The other monk was defrocked because he had not revealed his "sin" in the confessional. I was to remain, repent, and acquire therapy.

I remained, repented, missed my friend, and felt guilt for his dismissal. Six months passed. Nothing was said by my superior. I said my prayers and lived in a disillusioned state. Suddenly, one morning I was escorted to a local Catholic hospital and committed to the psychiatric ward for counterconditioning therapy. I was given ECT (electroconvulsive therapy), and aversive counterconditioning. The result was I never touched another monk (or anyone else for many years to come); remained in the Order (willing victim–the Reactive Wave) for one more year; and never ever went to confession again.

Later, I rose rapidly in the business world. At one research firm I was an executive, working long hours and the whole nine yards. My senior vice president tried to seduce me. He was surprised by my refusal. I arrived at work the following day, and the guards were told to not let me in. And on and on . . . .

The point? I will never return to the darkness of the closet, because the benefits (as addressed in this book) that I have received, overwhelm all the negatives.

The primary benefits I received are psycho-spiritual blessings. I have my integrity. In the end that is all there is. I know with certainty that my gayness is ontologically good. It is a gift, a benediction from God. Second, career-wise, I have developed a successful management consulting and training business in spite of corporate homophobia. Also, if closeted, I would have been lost in the mainstream of disempowering corporations, another nameless, closeted executive, just surviving. No thanks, I would rather thrive!

Once again, to take any journey involves risk. It is up to you. The greatest risk is the risk of introspection. To choose introspection is to venture forth into the "ma" state, the transitional bridge between Victimization and Manifestation. To choose introspection is to create your own vision through meditation, creative visualization, and active imagination. To choose introspection is to develop and activate a Proactive Wave Action Plan, the outcome of which is Actualization and Manifestation of the Self. To choose introspection is to choose individuation–a risky odyssey!

When we choose integrity through introspection we choose to go against the myths about the slain bodies of our gay brothers. To choose integrity does not bring with it a guarantee of safe passage. Just as Odysseus, we must fight the ancient gods and the "sirens" of discrimination and the violent winds of stereotyping. Gays do get fired! This book began with the first chapter entitled "The Need for the Journey." Its theme was "This is the way it is, accept it, and deal with it."

> The ultimate argument against the integrity of total honesty is that each of us knows someone who told the truth, did it in a nice way, and still got punished. That someone may even have been ourselves. The only answer to that is that "Yes, Virginia, organizations are unfair." (Block, 1987, p. 84)

However, the only other choice is to stay in the Reactive Wave, with ourselves being situationally dependent as willing victims living quiet lives of desperation. Unfortunately, we will discover, too late sometimes, that the so-called safe path was not safe at all.

Accepting, dealing with, and managing the risk of introspection is to choose the odyssey of integrity, and always requires courage and involves risk. The risks associated with introspection were tangentially touched on in Chapter 2 when I addressed the concept of "legitimate suffering." It is not surprising that my studies found—as did Jung's, Alder's, and more recently, M. Scott Peck's (1978)—that gays are like the population at large: introspection is indeed the road less traveled.

> "Oh how comforting it would be," Walt Whitman mused, "to run and live like animals who do not lie awake and worry about their souls." But there is no turning back, I cannot unsee what I have seen, cannot put uncertainties to rest merely because they are troubling, cannot cease asking questions that disturb my peace of mind. (Keen, 1983, p. 163)

Peck (1978) identifies four sub-risks associated with the basic risk of introspection. They are: the risk of loss; the risk of independence; the risk of commitment; and the risk of confrontation.

The first risk is the risk of vulnerability and loss. To choose introspection is to open oneself up. To open oneself up is to risk loss.

The Risk of Vulnerability and Loss

When we extend ourselves, our self enters new and unfamiliar territory, so to speak. Our self becomes a new and different self. We do things we are not accustomed to doing. We change.

The experience of change, of unaccustomed activity, of being on unfamiliar ground, of doing things differently is frightening. It always was and always will be. People handle their fear of change in different ways, but the fear is inescapable if they are in fact to change. Courage is not the absence of fear; it is the making of action in spite of fear, the moving out against the resistance engendered by fear into the unknown and into the future. (Peck, 1978, p. 131)

The process of introspection always includes risk-taking. However, if one does not embrace the risk and take the step, one never comes to that necessary mental shift, involvement in the situation, i.e., seeing, perceiving oneself as a part of and contributor to the situation. This perception is a necessary ingredient of empowerment. Paul Tillich (1952) wrote:

The courage to be is the ethical act in which man affirms his own being in spite of those elements of his existence which conflict with his essential self-affirmation . . . .

Courage is the affirmation of one's essential nature, one's inner aim or entelechy, but is an affirmation which has in itself the character of "in spite of" (pp. 3-4)

Again, Block (1986), p. 104 wrote:

Moving toward the frontier, creating a vision of greatness, demands an act of faith. Faith by its nature, is unmeasurable and indefensible through the use of data and external evidence. An act of faith moving toward a preferred future is a leap beyond what is now being experienced. This act of faith and act of courage are demanded of each of us if we wish to choose autonomy and put our survival into our own hands. (p. 104)

The second risk is the risk of independence, which is the foundation for the risk of interdependence as addressed in Chapter 4, relevant to empowerment.

The Risk of Independence and Interdependence

Thus all life itself represents a risk, and the more lovingly we live our lives the more risk we take. Of the thousands, maybe even millions, of risks we can take in a lifetime the greatest is the risk of growing up. Growing up is the act of stepping from childhood into adulthood. Actually it is more of a fearful leap than a step, and it is a leap that many people never really take in their lifetimes. Though they may outwardly appear to be adults, even successful adults perhaps, the majority of "grown-ups" remain until their death psychological children . . . . (Peck, 1978, p. 34)

This is the rite of passage, the severing of the shackles of childhood, to take the independent stand of the adolescent. Independence, once again, calls for courage because it requires self-esteem and self-governing, which so often gives one the sensation of being "out on a limb." However, it is this independence, this self-esteem and self-governing that becomes another major ingredient to the interdependence of gay empowerment.

Although Peck's work does not address interdependence, my research, as previously detailed, shows that interdependence and not independence is the state of adult-to-adult interaction. Interdependence is empowerment. However, the process is indeed developmental, starting with dependence, working through independence to actualizing and manifesting in interdependence.

The third risk is the risk of commitment. Introspection requires a strong commitment—making the promise to oneself and keeping it. The commitment is the courage to go beyond one's self, to extend love.

The Risk of Commitment

Whether it be shallow or not, commitment is the foundation, the bedrock of any genuinely loving relationship. Deep commitment does not guarantee the success of the relationship but does help more than any other factor to assure it. Initially shallow commitments may grow deep with time; if not, the relationship will likely crumble or else be inevitably sickly or chronically frail. Frequently we are not consciously aware of the immensity of the risk involved in making a deep commitment. (Peck, 1978, p. 140)

Although Peck is specifically addressing the concept of partnering, his words were echoed by many of those interviewed. The need for a strong commitment and loving relationship with self and with the gay community was reported by those interviewed. Once again, commitment requires courage and a willingness to go beyond oneself. Going beyond oneself requires that ability to see the inter-relationship between oneself and the situation. Commitment becomes another essential ingredient for gay empowerment. Commitment is the act of connecting; the act of trusting; and the act of carrying into deliberate action one's beliefs and values.

Covey (1989) refers to the developmental, inward-to-outward concept as: "Personal Victory proceeds Public Victory." Personal Victory requires that one makes a promise (commitment) to oneself and keeps it. Public Victory only comes after one has made the commitment to the inner work of introspection and keeps it in spite of the existential angst, thereby achieving the private victory of facing and managing the pain of existential suffering and building readiness for the public victory of empowerment.

The fourth risk is the risk of confrontation. Confrontation is the willingness to be a person-of-the-truth rather than a person-of-the-lie.

The Risk of Confrontation

This self-scrutiny, as objective as possible, is the essence of humility and meekness. In the words of an anonymous fourteenth-century British monk and spiritual teacher, "Meekness in itself, is nothing else than a true knowing and feeling of a man's self as he is. Any man who truly sees and feels himself as he is must surely be meek indeed."

There are, then, two ways to confront or criticize another human being: with instinctive and spontaneous certainty that one is right, or with a belief that one is probably right arrived at through scrupulous self-doubting and self-examination. The first is the way of arrogance; it is the most common way of parents, spouses, teachers, and people generally in their day-to-day affairs; it is usually unsuccessful, producing more resentment than growth and other effects that were not intended. The second is the way of humility; it is not common, requiring as it does a genuine extension of oneself; it is more likely to be successful, and it is never, in my experience, destructive. (Peck, 1978, p. 152)

What is being addressed here is the ability and willingness to confront one's values, beliefs, and perceptions. It is the process whereby one examines the filter through which one has been making sense out of one's milieu. It is the questioning of one's realm of reality. All of this, obviously, can be very psychologically painful. The outcome of such confrontation may be a need to change behavior. That behavior may be what has provided one with his "comfort zone" up to this point in his life. The danger of non-self-confrontation becomes apparent.

> To fail to confront when confrontation is required for the nurture of spiritual growth represents a failure to love equally as much as does thoughtless criticism or condemnation and other forms of active deprivation of caring. (Peck, 1978, p. 153)

IN SUMMARY

Chapter 1, "The Need for the Journey," outlined the purpose and the necessity of the odyssey from disempowerment to empowerment. Work and sexuality are not distinct species. An asexual work environment does not exist. Being gay is an issue whether one is closeted or actualized. Ignoring or denying these truths causes one to remain in the victim cycle. Seeing it, owning it, celebrating one's gayness is the only realistic and holistic approach. It is a necessity to move from disempowerment to empowerment or one simply lives a life of darkness–counterfeiting and counterfeiting, on and on.

Chapter 2, "This Is Where We Are," presented the business community paradigm–the gender of organizations is male, and the sexuality of organizations is heterosexual. No other paradigm is acceptable! The homosexual paradigm is at best tolerated. This dilemma postulates fundamental concepts that gays in organizations must accept as the reality of the starting point. One must know the beginning state before striving for the end state.

Chapter 3, "Drafting the Map," presented the Gay Model of Transition. The model illustrates the movement from disempowerment to empowerment, utilized by gay managers and executives who actualize and manifest their wholeness and integrity.

Chapter 4, "This Is Where We Must Go," provided distinctions and definitions to the components of the Gay Model of Transition. As the title indicates, this chapter described the promised land of Actualization and Manifestation.

This chapter, "On the Road," elaborated and expanded Chapter 4. The specific steps utilized by gay managers and executives who actualized and manifested their wholeness and integrity, and the Coactive Wave Action Plan, by stage of development, were delineated.

As we have completed the main body of this book, we have realized that the journey from disempowerment to empowerment is indeed the ancient Greek myth of the odyssey. It is also a journey similar to a spiritual transition from sleep to awareness to action. As in all spiritual transitions, the path from A to B is never linear. It is a spiral ascent. A spiral ascent permits revisiting so as to acquire insight and growth, movement ever upward. Odysseus' purpose and end state was clear. On the surface, he knows he wants to go home. Psychologically, he knows he must learn empowerment, because home is a state of integrity, actualized and manifested. Odysseus knows all this, yet he spent years on his way, developing his wholeness, doing his inner work so as to be able to do his outer work, on the circular island of spiritual and psychological growth and development where all roads go round and round.

If Odysseus and we gay managers and executives are on the road to empowerment, Actualization and Manifestation are in the process of what Thomas Moore calls "Soul-making."

> Soul-making is a journey that takes time, effort, skill, knowledge, intuition, and courage. It is helpful to know that all work with soul is process–alchemy, pilgrimage, and adventure–so that we do not expect instant success of even any kind of finality. All goals and all endings are heuristic, important in their being imagined, but never literally fulfilled. (Moore, 1992, p. 259)

Therefore, like home for Odysseus, Actualization and Manifestation is not a physical end point, but a state of being. It is a state of being whole. Wholeness is nourished by our integrity, as addressed throughout this book.

I believe, as we follow the path of the Gay Model of Transition laid out for us by our role models interviewed in this study, that we will be accessing our own inner power, as well as receiving the power in the universe that operates for peace, love, goodness, and abundance and that fosters oneness and therefore fulfillment.

> You can lose sight of oneness, but cannot make sacrifice of its reality. (*A Course in Miracles*, 1976, p. 543)

Credo in unum. I believe in one. The interdependence of the state of Actualization and Manifestation is based on the metaphysical reality that we are not separate. Dependence, codependence, and independence are illusions. Oneness is supported by integrity. Integrity is developed by the inner work of introspection and has brought you to the level of synergy (oneness)–Actualization and Manifestation. You are home, Odysseus!

Chapter 6, "The Travelog," is a summary that supports the research findings in Chapters 1 through 5.

Chapter 6

The Travelog:
Summary of Findings, Conclusions,
and Recommendations

You cannot make the Revolution.
You can only be the Revolution.

–Le Guin

This book is a product of an almost lifelong journey. The book grew out of a lifetime of personal growth and experience as a gay executive, as well as over 20 years of organizational psychology consulting and training. In my role as an organizational psychologist, I have consulted with and trained executives all over America in small and large corporations. Where are the gay managers and executives? A nagging question. Furthermore, if they are there, how did they get there; what compromises, if any, did they have to make; and were they able to maintain their integrity and wholeness as gays? These questions needed to be answered.

Furthermore, the Union Institute was the only university I could find that would permit and support a doctoral study about gay managers and executives. From 1984 to 1987, the university became the umbrella under which such an intensive, scrutinized study occurred. Next, a second round of interviews of an additional 20 gay managers and executives occurred from 1991 to 1994. A second review of relevant literature also took place during this time frame.

The purpose of this chapter is to present a summary of the findings from the research conducted during the study. Furthermore, this chapter ends by discussing major conclusions and recommendations for further investigation.

The chapter is organized as follows:

- Methodology;
- Presentation of Data, Interpretation, and Observations;
- Conclusions and Recommendations.

METHODOLOGY

The data collected for this study were to examine the movement of gay males from disempowerment to empowerment (Actualization and Manifestation) within the heterosexual corporate world. The perspective of this study is to test out or understand why and how, rather than to *prove*; that is, the objective of this effort was to understand why and how gay males in business firms deal with issues of difference. To do so, the study relies more on qualitative than strictly quantitative research methods.

Research Methods

The research methods I used include the following:

- Heuristic Study;
- Literature Review;
- Pattern of Reaction Survey; and
- In-depth Interviews.

A Heuristic Study of My Own Experience

Heuristics is a relatively new method of research. One's experiences within one's environment are considered "hard" data. Heuristics is a rigorous system requiring retreats dedicated solely to introspection. Data collected from this introspection must be methodically reported.

For my study, I arranged two retreats, both one week each. I began my day by practicing relaxation and meditation techniques.

The goal of the first retreat was to discover what had happened to me: What was my experience? Each day was dedicated to a review and examination of a specific period of my work life. I kept journals by decade, including my feelings, anecdotes, and observations.

The need for a second retreat resulted from reading the literature on human empowerment. In *Transition*, Adams, Hayes, and Hapson, (1976) had presented to me the possibility of expanding my model. Adams' model is sequentially immobilization, minimization, depression, acceptance of reality and letting-go, testing, searching for meaning, and internalization.

I also needed to examine Elisabeth Kübler-Ross's (1969) ideas of positive growth and the stages she described in *Death and Dying*. Not that being gay equates with dying, but the attitudes and strategies one uses under adversity such as dying may correlate with the attitudes and strategies of gays trying to thrive in corporate America. Ross's model progressively is: denial (after shock), anger, bargaining, depression, and acceptance. Adams' and Kübler-Ross's models were the primary developmental strategies examined during the heuristic study. Other developmental models that were examined were:

- Carl Jung's developmentally determined dimension of psychological growth and interjecture from the extroversion of youth to the introversion of adulthood;
- Lawrence Kohlberg's theory of ethical development which suggests an invariable sequence of stages: preconventional (self-centered); conventional (avoid disapproval); and postconventional (universal ethical principles orientation);
- Roger Walsh and Frances Vaughan's six common elements of transcendence: ethics; attentional training; emotional transformation; motivation; refining awareness; and wisdom.
- Stephen Covey's study of the habits of effective people–private victories of: being proactive, beginning with the end in mind, and putting first things first; public victories of: thinking win/win, seeking first to understand, then to be understood, and creative cooperation; and renewal strategies of: balance, self-renewal, and working inside-out.

- Kathryn Cramer's personal change dynamics: challenge (opportunities vs. dangers); empowerment (exploration and invention) and transformation (enhancement).

I devoted introspection and meditation to their ideas. My journal was kept around the models: did I experience these stages? to what extent? how did I feel? The model of transition presented in this book is the result of the two heuristic retreats and the 40 interviews.

A Review of the Scholarly Literature

In addition to the traditional field of organizational psychology, the review of scholarly literature included: transpersonal psychology; gay studies; creative visualization; and empowerment strategies. A review of the literature revealed few published studies regarding gay males in the corporate environment. Although descriptive, biographical studies have been completed, I found nothing that presented models, steps, or strategies to move from disempowerment to empowerment. I also found nothing that focused on the strategies used specifically by gay managers and executives. The literature reviewed is listed in the reference notes at the end of the book.

Patterns of Reaction Survey

A survey to measure the patterns of reactions at various stages of development from disempowerment to empowerment was developed and administered. Because of the sensitive nature of the survey, I wanted the sample population to be as large as possible. Two hundred gay male managers were surveyed.

Sampling is always a problematic issue. It is even more so when dealing with the nebulous group called "the gay community." The gay community does not have boundaries. It is not a coherent group, etc., let alone "gay businessmen." Without a "list" of the population at large there was no way that any researcher could *simply* do a statistical sample.

Therefore, identification and selection of subjects was a long and cautious effort. The primary source was the National Business

Council affiliates (gay and lesbian business and professional associations). Also, my extensive consulting contacts proved invaluable. However, once trust was developed between me and the first line of contacts, they in turn provided referrals. Referrals brought more referrals, etc. Demographics of the respondents are found in this chapter under Basic Findings from the 200 Surveys.

As previously stated, to target individuals to survey, I drew upon the services of National Business Council affiliates located in Washington, DC, Baltimore, New York City, Seattle, Los Angeles, and San Francisco. In New York and San Francisco, local contacts who were familiar with my research project hand-distributed the questionnaire to men they knew worked at the managerial level. The Greater Washington Business and Professional Council also screened prospective respondents for managerial level. Also, in Washington, DC, Mr. James Russler, to whom this book is dedicated, hand-distributed numerous questionnaires. Many first-line contacts volunteered to hand-distribute questionnaires.

The purpose of the first four questions of the survey was to establish demographic information. The remaining questions were formed to reflect, as much as possible, the key stages in the model of transition. Two open-ended questions were included to obtain descriptive information about the various stages experienced by the respondents. (A copy of the survey questionnaire is appended to the end of this section of this chapter.) A breakdown of the results of the survey is found later in the chapter under Presentation of Data.

In-Depth Interviews

In-depth interviews with 40 gay managers/executives were conducted. Twenty interviews were drawn from among those who completed the survey questionnaires from 1984 to 1987. They volunteered to be interviewed; in a sense, they selected themselves.

An additional 20 interviews were conducted from 1991 to 1994. These interviewees did not complete the Patterns of Reaction Survey. These individuals were identified and selected through referrals. The subjects were:

• All college educated;
• Middle to upper-middle class;

- Managerial/executive experience ranged from two years to 21 years;
- Age ranged from 30 to 50; and
- Twenty-five were white and five were African American.

Confidentiality and secrecy clearly frustrated the aim of this work. Perhaps that is the "existential suffering" that must be endured by those of us who wish to study our gay brothers. Three men of the latter 20 volunteered and were willing to see their names and opinions in this book. However, that would be statistically and ethically inappropriate, because I began the study guaranteeing anonymity.

In the text, I cloaked all the men. I did not refer to pseudonyms. Furthermore, I did not use company names, although all qualify as Fortune 500 companies. I have made every effort, however, to present the truth of the circumstances and the facts of the events while maintaining confidentiality. Because of my strict adherence to confidentiality, willingness to speak about my own experiences as a gay executive, and experiences with the business community, I believe the level of candor and trust, the foundation of any in-depth interview, was very high. Therefore, the depth of what was revealed is indeed valid.

Interviews were conducted in one-on-one sessions ranging from one to two hours. The interviews were conducted over lunch or dinner, or in after-business sessions. *No respondent* agreed/found it convenient to be interviewed at his business office. (This, in and of itself, may or may not reflect the "comfort zone" of Isolation and Retreat.) Individuals who were in the Proactive Wave wanted to talk and to ask questions. Individuals in the Reactive Wave wanted only to complain or to object to the study; on the whole, they had less to say.

The interviews consisted of four parts: (1) general comments to set the climate and to reassure the interviewee; (2) assurance of confidentiality and anonymity. (It is interesting to note that all of those interviewed raised the second point before I could.) There was a generally held disbelief that a gay male could not remain anonymous; they felt that somehow when the data were tabulated they could be individually identified; (3) explanation of my process: that the study was not a "cause/problem" study; that I began with the assumption that homosexuality was healthy; and (4) the interview questions.

Two questions were explored: (1) interviewees were asked whether they were out of the closet; and (2) they were asked to share their experiences as gay males in a heterosexual business organization. Results of the interviews are found later in the chapter under Presentation of Data.

Limitations

The study is limited to gay males, minority inclusive, in the business environment. Groups such as lesbians and government and private agencies are excluded, as previously outlined. The location of the sample is geographically limited to six urban areas: three on the East Coast and three on the West Coast of the United States.

Because of the sensitive nature of the interviews, and because the surveys and in-depth interviews were voluntary, there may be some selective bias in the sample population. Some men were guarded in their comments; some may have falsified answers. No attempt was made to verify information received.

The working of the survey questionnaire caused some ambiguities. One of the demographic questions asked for "present position" rather than directly asking, "Are you a manager?" Some respondents described job function rather than indicating their titles. Question 9 was included to substantiate Question 6. There was no correlation between the answers to these two questions, possibly because of the phrasing of Question 9. Problems between expected answers and actual answers to survey questions are dealt with in the presentation of data section.

Audience

The audience for this study is gay male managers and executives. The descriptive states and models of the applied research effort are directed toward sharing other gay males' productive experiences of positive integration. While business organizations may find this study enlightening and useful for training and human resource development, it was not the purpose of this effort.

Analyses

Heuristic Study and Reading of the Literature. An *analysis* of my heuristic study and my reading should not be separated from the *results* of my heuristic study and my reading. I looked inside myself–at everything that had been settled in me–like sifting through the layers of the ocean floor. This process cannot be compartmentalized, or at least it is not wise to try to compartmentalize it within the confines of this book. I therefore chose to describe the results of my heuristic study and my reading here, because in many ways the results are the analysis.

The Stages of Transition Model had its roots in the early heuristic phase of the study. It emerged from the intrapersonal question, "What has been my experience?" The exploration of what I had personally experienced in my professional career occurred during a rigorous retreat. The answer to the question was a four-stage model of (1) *denial* that sexual orientation was a factor for discrimination; (2) *anger* that sexual orientation was indeed used to prevent advancement in the organization; (3) *isolation* from the sociopolitical dynamics of the organization; and finally (4) segregation then *integration* back into the mainstream functions of the organization.

The major themes that emerged from the first heuristic study were the transition waves (an attempt to establish when and in what sequences each of the four stages occurred) and the delineation of the states of disempowerment and empowerment.

The second step in the development of the model was to research transition and empowerment literature. A search within the gay-specific literature proved fruitless, i.e., although many had written about how to "come out," none, to my knowledge, had addressed "stages" of growth or development for gay managers and executives.

The third step was a search within the generic field of human potential literature. This search led me to the works of Adams, Hayes, and Hapson, *Transition* (1976), and Elisabeth Kübler-Ross, *On Death and Dying* (1969) and others delineated earlier in this chapter. However Adams' and Kübler-Ross's works were the primary force.

In *Transition*, Adams, Hayes, and Hapson, (1976) presented the possibility of more than four stages in my transition process. Kübler-Ross (1969) advanced the idea that choosing to "let go" could result in positive, personal growth; the stages she described of reconciling one's self to death seemed to have paralleled my "coming out." These works caused a serious reconsideration of my initial four-stage model.

The fourth and final step was to once again rigorously scrutinize my personal experience. After testing myself against Adams' model, Kübler-Ross's model, and my own model which had resulted from the previous rigorous retreat–I intensely realized that my odyssey toward the desired state of Actualization and Manifestation had entailed additional stages. Out of the whole experience came the model presented here, my own personal stages of transition from disempowerment to empowerment.

This study discusses the model in a "triangulatory" fashion, that is, an assembled composite view of my heuristic study, the review of the pertinent literature, and the experiences of the interviewees.

Pattern of Reactions Survey. The purpose of the survey was to collect demographic data; to eliminate any respondents from the study who were not managers or executives in a heterosexual, business organization; to ascertain concrete data regarding the respondent's position in the model of transition and how he felt about that position. (See Figure 6.1.) Demographic information was tabulated to establish the average age and the percentage of white and black gay males.

Questions 1, 2, and 3 established whether a respondent was a manager or executive and whether he worked for a straight-owned and -operated organization. The purpose of essay Questions 4 and 5 was a check and balance mechanism in relation to Question 6. I dealt with the responses to the essay questions by cross-referencing the responses to Questions 4 and 5 with the item checked in Question 6 (stage in the Model of Transition). This was done to verify that the respondent was, indeed, in the stage he said he was. The essay Questions 4 and 5 yielded no significant anecdotal data. Question 6 was used to collect the hard data regarding the respondent's position on the Model of Transition.

FIGURE 6.1. The Pattern of Reactions Survey

Date:_____
Age:_____
Race:____White
_____African American
_____Other

1. Please describe, within the boundaries of confidentiality, your present position within your organization.

2. Is the organization that you work for primarily:

    _____ Gay
    _____ Straight

3. Are you "out" at work?

    _____ Yes
    _____ No

    A. If yes, how did that occur?

    B. If no, are there individuals at work who know that you are gay?

    _____ Yes
    _____ No

    B1. If yes, what percentage of them are:

    –Gay   _____ %
    –Straight   _____ %

    B2. What percentage of the above gay individuals are

    –totally out at work   _____ %
    –out to a limited number of people   _____ %

4. Please describe your experiences of being a gay male within your business environment.

5. Please describe any incident, in any position in your career, wherein being gay became a conflict issue.

    A. Please describe how you coped, dealt with, and/or managed the above situation.

6. Please check the statement which <u>best</u> describes how you view your current work situation:

_____ A. My being gay has nothing at all to do with my work situation.

_____ B. I do not believe my being gay will affect how those with whom I work view my performance. Nevertheless, I do not draw attention to it.

_____ C. It is a constant struggle to prevent people in my organization from using my being gay against me.

_____ D. I am unable to prevent people in my organization from treating me in a negative fashion, due to my sexual preference.

_____ E. People in my organization accept that I am gay; it is no longer an issue that affects me on the job.

_____ F. I am in a position to assist others dealing with the issues that arise from being gay in their organization.

7. I find my current job situation, as described in Question 6:

_____ A. Intolerable

_____ B. Troublesome

_____ C. Acceptable

_____ D. Satisfying

8. Given my job situation, as described in Question 6:

_____ A. There is little I expect to be able to do to change it.

_____ B. I would very much like to change it, but do not know how.

_____ C. I am actively attempting to change it.

_____ D. I neither need nor want to change it.

FIGURE 6.1 (continued)

9. Please check all statements below, *other than the one checked in Question 6*, which have applied to you in the past, on the job.

_____ A. My being gay has nothing at all to do with my work situation.

_____ B. I do not believe my being gay will affect how those with whom I work view my performance; nevertheless, I do not draw attention to it.

_____ C. It is a constant struggle to prevent people in my organization from using my being gay against me.

_____ D. I am unable to prevent people in my organization from treating me in a negative fashion, due to my sexual preference.

_____ E. People in my organization accept that I am gay; it is no longer an issue that affects me on the job.

_____ F. I am in a position to assist others to deal with the issues that arise from being gay in their organization.

In-Depth Interviews. The purpose of the interviews was not to gather "hard" data, but to obtain anecdotal accounts of the respondents' experiences. Their stories were examined for indicators of the transitional stages they had gone through and the stage they were presently in. I used my own professional judgment to reach conclusions from their inference. For example, those in Co and Proactive stages were really interested in the study and wanted to help; those in the Reactive stage were angry or tried to persuade me the study was not prudent.

Organization of Material

My approach to organizing my materials in order to present them in this research paper is through the process of triangulation. The three angles are: the heuristic data, the research of the literature, and the results of the surveys and interviews. The analysis and results of the data appear in this sequence. Each angle served as its own support, and the convergence became this book. Diagram 6.1 illustrates the process.

Throughout this book, I have attempted to present the data and my ideas in a convergence fashion. Chapter 1 and Chapter 2 focus on the heuristic data and the research on the literature. Chapter 3 is the convergence and intertwining of these with the information and ideas gleaned from the surveys and interviews. Chapters 4 and 5 describe strategies and action steps gleaned from principals, heuristic data, and literature sources. The goal of Chapter 6 is to present "numbers" to back up the theses contained in Chapter 4 and to illustrate the problems and issues discussed in Chapter 1 through 5.

Several themes emerged from the survey and interviews. These themes were correlated with the heuristic revelations and my review of the literature. These themes are interwoven into the whole of the book. However, I have isolated several for discussion in this chapter, under Conclusions.

PRESENTATION OF DATA, INTERPRETATION, AND OBSERVATIONS

The purpose of this section is to present findings from the research conducted during my study of gay males' transition in the workplace, not methodology. The section presents basic data from

DIAGRAM 6.1. Organization of Materials

Heuristic

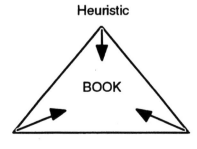

Literature   Principals (Surveys and Interview)

each method–the heuristic study and readings, the 200 surveys, and the 40 in-depth interviews. The section assembles relevant data, includes observations, and draws inferences where appropriate. Conclusions will be presented at the end of this chapter.

BASIC FINDINGS FROM THE HEURISTIC STUDY

The first retreat yielded the realization that I had experienced a four-stage process in my personal journey from disempowerment to empowerment. They were: Denial, Anger, Isolation, and Attempt to Integrate.

The second retreat yielded the present Model of Transition. I compared Adams, Hayes, and Hapson's (1976) Self-Esteem Changes During Transition and Kübler-Ross's (1969) Stages of Death and Dying with my initial four-stage model as well as the other models cited earlier in this chapter. Diagram 6.2 illustrates this comparison.

DIAGRAM 6.2. Initial Model Comparison

Adams, Hayes, and Hapson	Kübler-Ross	Miller
1. Immobilization	1. Denial	1. Denial
2. Minimization (Denial)	2. Anger	2. Anger
3. Depression (and Anger)	3. Bargaining	3. Isolation
4. Acceptance of Reality and Letting Go	4. Depression	4. Attempt to Integrate
5. Testing	5. Acceptance	
6. Search for Meaning		
7. Internalization		

Results of the comparison:

Matches between my model and theirs:

1. Immobilization and Minimization (Adams, Hayes, and Hapson), Denial (Kübler-Ross).
2. Depression (and Anger) (Adams, Hayes, and Hapson), Anger (Kübler-Ross), and Anger (Miller).
3. Depression (Adams, Hayes, and Hapson), Depression (Kübler-Ross), and Isolation (Miller).
4. Acceptance of Reality and Letting Go (Adams, Hayes, and Hapson), Acceptance (Kübler-Ross), and Attempt to Integrate (Miller).

Gaps between my model and theirs:

1. Testing (Adams, Hayes, and Hapson), and Bargaining (Kübler-Ross).
2. Search for Meaning and Internalization (Adams, Hayes, and Hapson).

After giving serious consideration to the gaps, I realized that I had indeed experienced those stages but not in an order parallel to their models. The outcome to the second retreat was my six-stage transitional model, wherein other models cited earlier were included. (See Diagram 6.3.)

BASIC FINDINGS FROM THE 200 SURVEYS

The results from the "Pattern of Reactions Surveys" are presented in the following categories:

- Demographic Variables;
- Respondents' Stage in the Transition Cycle;
- Respondents' Attitudes Toward Their Stage in the Transition Cycle; and
- Respondents' Transitional Patterns.

Demographic Variables

Questions 1, 2, and 3 of the survey measure demographics. The sample for this study was 200 gay male managers and executives within straight businesses and industries. Their positions varied from first level supervisors to executive level vice presidents. The business and industries varied from banking to telecommunications firms.

DIAGRAM 6.3. Gay Model of Transition

	STAGE	WAVE	STRATEGY	OUTCOME
I.	Denial and Minimization	REACTIVE Self as a result of the situation	C O P I	Situationally Dependent
II.	Retreat and Isolation		N G	
III.	Anger and Conflict			
IV.	Depression and Victimization			
V.	Internalization and Transformation	PROACTIVE Self as part of the situation	D E A L I N G	Integration of Self in Situation
VI.	Actualization and Manifestation	COACTIVE Self as instrumental in the situation	M A N A G I N G	Synergy of Self and Situation

The geographic area was limited to three East and three West Coast cities of the United States. Table 6.1 portrays distribution of surveys by city. New York and San Francisco were the primary target cities (80 percent of the total sample) because of their large gay populations and their concentration of large corporations resulting in a higher likelihood of gay managers.

The average age of the respondents was 39. One hundred ninety-four respondents were white gay males (94 percent), and six respondents were African-American gay males (3 percent). One hundred percent of the respondents worked for organizations that were primarily operated by the heterosexual community *Fortune 500* companies.

Respondent's Stage in the Transition Model

The intent of the open-ended Questions 4 and 5 was that of check and balance with Question 6. Did the responses to Question 4 and 5 match the checked item (stage in the Transition Model) in Question 6?

Within certain limitations Questions 4 and 5 matched Question 6 by 96 percent (168) of the 172 people who completed the question appropriately. Four percent (4) of the responses did not correlate to the item checked in Question 6. The limitations were 3 percent (6 individ-

TABLE 6.1. Demographics

City	No. of Subjects	% of Subjects
Washington, DC	22	11
Baltimore	5	2.5
New York	73	36.5
Seattle	3	1.5
Los Angeles	12	6
San Francisco	85	42.5
TOTAL	200	100%

uals) marked the question N/A; 11 percent (5 individuals) did not complete the question; and 86 percent (172) completed the question appropriately. The open-ended questions did not yield any directly useful anecdotal data for use in this study.

Question 6 ("Please check the statement which *best* describes how you view your current work situation") is meant to determine which state the respondent was in at the time of the completion of the survey. Table 6.2 illustrates the results of Question 6.

–Only 6 percent of the respondents see themselves as Coactive. This stage requires a transformational shift in consciousness, beliefs, values, and perceptions, a profound transmutation of previous perceptions of the self, viewing the self as instrumental in the situation.

–Thirteen percent of the respondents see themselves as Proactive. This is a time of self-remembering in a social-systemic manner. Herein is where one truly begins to contemplate a mental shift in consciousness, values, beliefs, and perceptions that will lead to a vision of reality in which being gay means being whole, good, and eventually Coactive.

–Eighty-one percent of the respondents see themselves as Reactive. In this wave one views one's self as dependent upon a situation which is seen as something totally outside one's sphere of influence. Sixty-four percent are "closeted" at work and thus in Denial and Minimization (35 percent) and Retreat and Isolation (29 percent) stages. Only 11 percent of the respondents were in the Anger and Conflict stage and only 6 percent were in the Depression and Victimization stage.

The results from Question 6, especially the breakdown of the various stages within the Reactive Wave, were unexpected. Although this book does not attempt to address why some gay men are in one stage and others in another, I would have guessed, from my background and direct experience, and the cultural changes of the 1960s and 1970s, that of those in the Reactive Wave fewer men would have been in the closet in 1987 and more would have been in the Anger and Conflict stage. Given the openness of the Clinton

TABLE 6.2. Gay Male Managers' Views of Current Work Situation

Question 6: Please check the statement which best describes how you view your current work situation.

Wave	No. of Respondents	% of Respondents	% By Item and Stage	
REACTIVE Self as a result of the situation	70	35%	A. My being gay has nothing at all to do with my work situation.	I. Denial and Minimization
	58	29%	B. I do not believe my being gay will affect how those with whom I work view my performance. Nevertheless I do not draw attention to it.	II. Retreat and Isolation
	22	11%	C. It is a constant struggle to prevent people in my organization from using my being gay against me.	III. Anger and Conflict
	12	6%	D. I am unable to prevent people in my organization from treating me in a negative fashion, due to my sexual preference.	IV. Depression and Victimization
Total	162	81%		
PROACTIVE Self as a part of the situation	26	13%	E. People in my organization accept that I am gay; it is no longer an issue which affects me on the job.	V. Internalization and Transformation
Total	26	13%		
COACTIVE Self as instrumental in the situation	12	6%	F. I am in a position to assist others to deal with the issues that arise from being gay in their organizations.	VI. Actualization and Manifestation
Total	12	6%		

137

Administration and the greater number who participated in the 1993 March on Washington, one would have expected, if the survey were to be administered again, to have higher levels in the Coactive Wave. However, the business world is still the last great closet.

It is surprising, even after the activism of the 1960s and 1970s, when such leaders as Harvey Milk, a city councilman for San Francisco, and Wall Street broker David Goodstein, were successful in getting gays to come out, that such a high percentage of my sample was still in the closet. Next, 23 cities in the U.S. now have gay Professional and Business Council chapters. Their existence and their goals would have resulted, in the opinion of the writer, in fewer individuals in the Reactive Wave.

Respondents' Attitudes Toward Their Stage in the Model of Transition

Question 7 provides positive and negative indicators to determine how the respondents felt about their present stage. Table 6.3 presents the overall data. Table 6.4 presents the data correlated to the wave.

Negative feelings were expressed more frequently by respondents in the Reactive Wave than by those in any other wave. Those

TABLE 6.3. Levels of Job Satisfaction for Gay Male Managers

Question 7: I find my current job situation, as described in Question 6:

Poles	No. of Respondents	% of Respondents	Indicators
Negative	14	7	A. Intolerable
	26	13	B. Troublesome
Positive	36	18	C. Acceptable
	124	62	D. Satisfying

- 80% of the respondents felt positive about their present stage in the Transition Model relative to their current job situation.
- 61% of the Reactive Wave (81% of the total population) felt positive about their situation.
- 98% of the Proactive Wave (13% of the total population) felt positive about their situation.
- 100% of the Coactive Wave (6% of the total population) felt positive about their situation.

TABLE 6.4. Level of Job Satisfaction for Gay Male Managers

Question 7: I find my current job situation as described in Question 6:

Wave	Indicators	No. of Respondents	% of Respondents	Poles
REACTIVE Self as a result of the situation	A. Intolerable	11	7%	Negative
	B. Troublesome	52	32%	(39%)
	C. Acceptable	91	56%	Positive
	D. Satisfying	8	5%	(61%)
PROACTIVE Self as a part of the situation	A. Intolerable	0	0%	Negative
	B. Troublesome	1	1%	(2%)
	C. Acceptable	6	22%	Positive
	D. Satisfying	19	76%	(98%)
COACTIVE Self as instrumental in the situation	A. Intolerable	0	0%	Negative
	B. Troublesome	0	0%	(0%)
	C. Acceptable	0	0%	Positive
	D. Satisfying	12	100%	(100%)

in the Coactive Wave, on the other hand, expressed total satisfaction with their current job situation. The inference that can be drawn from Questions 6 and 7 combined is that 61 percent of the respondents in the "self as a result of the situation" wave expressed positive feelings about their job situation. It would seem from this finding that many gays are, in truth, "willing victims" of their own negative self-concept. Table 6.5 presents the data obtained from

TABLE 6.5. Gay Male Managers' Attitudes Toward Change in Job Situation

Question 8: Given my job situation, as described in Question 6:

A.	There is little I expect to be able to do to change it.	46	23%
B.	I would very much like to change it, but do not know how.	4	2%
C.	I am actively attempting to change it.	8	4%
D.	I neither need nor want to change it.	142	71%

- 71% of the respondents saw no need to change their job situation—either because the job situation suited them or their purpose, or they were indifferent.

- 25% of the respondents, however, expressed an inability to bring about change.

Question 8 regarding managers' attitudes toward change in their job situation.

Respondents' Transitional Patterns

Question 9 was designed to ascertain if respondents move through the transitional model in a sequential manner, as I had done, and if a fully integrated process required movement through all six stages.

As previously mentioned in the Methodology section, Question 9 was not able to fulfill its purpose. Movement through the transitional cycle cannot be ascertained from the data. (See limitations expressed in the Methodology section.)

BASIC FINDINGS FROM THE 40 IN-DEPTH INTERVIEWS

The purpose of the in-depth interview was to acquire anecdotal data regarding:

- What gay males have experienced as members of straight business organizations; and

- What enablers operate which permit gay males to continue to move toward employment?

Two questions were explored:

1. Interviewees were asked whether they were out of the closet. One hundred percent (40 respondents) responded yes.
2. Interviewees were asked to share their experiences as gay males in a straight business organization.
    –The response to this question became the quotes from confidential interviews, contained in Chapters 3, 4, and 5, as well as in the conclusion of Chapter 6.

Additional findings not previously described are:

1. From my professional viewpoint:
    –Twenty percent (8 interviewees) were in the Reactive Wave as exhibited by behavior of anger toward me because the study would be dangerous to gay males. Their attitude was one of "Certain things are better left untouched" (confidential interview).
    –Eighty percent (32 interviewees) were in the Proactive and Coactive Waves as exhibited by their excitement and interest. They freely described their experiences, made suggestions, asked questions, and asked for copies of the study once it was completed.
2. The 40 in-depth interviews yielded data that would indicate that those who did not experience Stages III (Anger and Conflict) and IV (Depression and Minimization) did, however, combine the stages of Retreat and Isolation with the Internalization and Transformation stage. In addition, interviewees described techniques similar to Creative Visualization, and Active Imagination, elaborated on in Chapter 3, to facilitate their movement into the Actualization and Manifestation stage.
3. Eighty percent (32 interviewees) shared the enablers, that is, techniques that permitted them to continue to move toward empowerment. They were:
    –Each had to purposefully work on deepening self-trust and self-esteem. (Risks Associated with Introspection, Chapter 6, and Self-Image Concepts, Chapter 4.)

–Each had role models and belonged to a support group. (Role Models and Support Systems, Chapter 6, and, in Chapter 6, concepts of transcending sexual orientation, stereotypes, and support groups.)

–Each had practiced some form of outcome thinking. (Creative Visualization, Chapter 4, and the ability to view negative experiences as positive learning and actualization opportunities, Chapter 6.)

SUMMARY OF THE STUDY

The study set out to address three questions using different methodologies described in depth in the previous section. As in all cases of true questioning, one never knows what he will find. The investigator can merely ask the question and wait for the reply. The answer may be completely unanticipated or may not be forthcoming at all.

–What have gay males experienced as members of straight business organizations?

Gay males have had experiences which paralleled mine. The descriptions of experiences gathered in the in-depth interviews matched mine at different stages discovered through my heuristic study. This anecdotal data is found in Chapters 3, 4, and 5 describing appropriate stages of the Transition Model. No evidence of progression through the model was sought nor encountered in the interviews.

–Does the Model of Transition from disempowerment to empowerment, formed by my own experiences, hold true for others?

The interviews indicate it holds true in that others have experienced and described similar stages. The survey instrument was designed to test the whole model. Question 6 determined the stage the individual was in at the time of the survey and Question 9 was to determine if he progressed in sequence through all the stages to his current one. Because of the limitations of the Pattern of Reactions Survey (Methodology) I can only say that others experienced similar stages, but there is no hard data to indicate whether there is a progression through stages and whether the progression is one I had experienced.

—What enablers operate which permit gay males to move toward empowerment?
The data on enablers comes from my own experience and from both the in-depth interviews and Question 5.A of the Survey. Those respondents who were on the move toward empowerment described the enablers portrayed in Chapter 5.

As is often the case, the conclusions transcend the question asked. A greater amount and variety of information was gathered than was sought. The next section presents and explores my conclusions.

CONCLUSIONS AND RECOMMENDATIONS

Homosexuality in the business community is still largely an uninvestigated problem. The reader has simply to check the selected bibliography of this study, compiled by a computer search at the Library of Congress, to find that little of substance has been written on this subject.

Corporations do not generally recognize the presence of homosexual businessmen (Zoglin, 1979). To complicate the effort of studying the gay manager or executive, gays in business, unlike other minorities, are largely invisible. In the early stages of this study, I spent a great deal of time and effort studying equal rights (people of color, women) movements in the business community. However, the "invisibility" variable was significant enough to make me drop my attempt to do a comparison among these groups.

Most gay managers and executives wish to remain indistinguishable from their colleagues and are reluctant to discuss any differences. It is difficult to impossible to get hard facts and statistics on gays in business.

Getting hard facts and statistics on homosexuals in business is a difficult task. Even the most liberated gay executive—one whose homosexuality is common knowledge in the company—is very cautious about discussing the subject with an outsider. Getting information on the large-scale incidence of homosexuality in business is almost impossible. Since no data are kept on the subject, all we can do is rely on the more-or-less educated guesses of homosexual executives themselves. (Zoglin, 1979, p. 69)

Even the most open gay executives in this study were very, very cautious in discussing the impact of their homosexuality in their business environment. Thirty-seven individuals interviewed stipulated that neither their name nor the names of their companies be published, although this was specifically stated by me numerous times.

During the in-depth interviews, all 40 individuals assertively shared their disbelief in the concept of confidentiality and anonymity! All carried with them examples of how they had been "subjects" or their friends had been "subjects" of studies in which data that led directly back to them had been shared. Thus, there was great reluctance on the part of even those who were out of the closet to deal with issues of "too much exposure."

> I think you'll find in your study that most of us who believe ourselves to be out of the closet still carry around inside us our own brand of "homophobia." I believe that most of the gay executives I know wrongly believe that if gay people kept their homosexuality private, they would probably be a lot better off. It is true to say that most homosexuals make every effort, from dress to mannerisms, to remain indistinguishable from heterosexuals. Your study may threaten that belief and therefore you will probably find it difficult indeed to get hard facts. (confidential interview)

Conclusions

A major conclusion can be drawn from the difficult task of researching this study and from the in-depth interviews. *Corporations and gay executives, sadly, are content with homosexuals staying in the closet.* The data from the 200 surveys indicated that 81 percent of the respondents were in the Reactive Wave at the time of the survey. This is not a positive conclusion; however, it is a realistic conclusion from which recommendations and further studies may flow.

A second conclusion drawn from this study is that *every aspect of the gay male's business life is colored by the way he views his own homosexuality.* If his perception of himself mirrors the myth of white, heterosexual, male supremacy, which remains etched in the American business psyche, he will remain stuck in the Reactive Wave–disempowered. If, on the other hand, his view of his homosexuality is that it is good, distinctive, and additive to the business community, he is able to reach the levels of Actualization and Manifestation discussed in this study.

Mark Freedman (1975a) refers to this positive self-image as "centering."

> Many gay people have responded to social pressures against homosexuality by "centering." By discovering and living according to their own values. An intense quest for identity, purpose, and meaning often begins quite early, certainly by the time young homosexuals begin to appreciate the tremendous social pressures against them. (p. 30)

All individuals who had arrived at the stage of Actualization and Manifestation had used some form of creative visualization. Being able to actively hold on to a vision of what they wanted life to be became a key variable. Unless gays are able to see themselves as "chosen people," they will continue to act as "slaves" to the finite power games of the corporations.

Stereotyping of sex roles and sexual orientation is common in organizations. This research inadvertently discovered what Alice Sargent (Ed., 1977) and others address in *Beyond Sex Roles*, and what Mark Freedman (1975b) addresses as society's denigration of unconventional behavior. Dr. Freedman found that over 90 percent of the people questioned about the attributes of a mentally healthy person devalued "feminine" traits; they considered most "female" characteristics, such as gentleness, neither socially nor psychologically valuable for either men or women. They (wrongly) believed that homosexuals embody all that is offensive about femininity.

Support groups are the primary mechanism for moving out of the state of denial about one's sexuality and its impact on the organization. As previously stated, over 80 percent of those interviewed felt that coming to grips with their sexuality and coming out was pain equal to abandonment. It was only in the presence of those who had come out that individuals were able to overcome their fears of abandonment and find support and security. The *I Ching* addresses support groups as T'ung Jin, Fellowship with Men.

> Fellowship with men in the open succeeds. True fellowship among men must be based upon a concern that is universal. That is why it is said that fellowship with men in the open succeeds. If unity of this kind prevails, even difficult tasks can be accomplished. (1950, p. 56)

The ability to view negative experiences as positive learning and actualization opportunities is a necessary skill for moving from disempowerment to empowerment. Individuals who were able to ask the questions, "What can I learn from this and how can I make this an opportunity for growth and advancement?" were able to make a transition. However, being able to ask the questions at all required that the individuals be in the Proactive Wave of their transition.

For myself, THE MAJOR CONCLUSION IS THAT MOVING FROM DENIAL AND MINIMIZATION TO ACTUALIZATION AND MANIFESTATION CAN BE DONE. Six percent (12) of respondents to the surveys, and 80 percent (32) of interviewees, as well as myself, have completed the odyssey. What was common to the 45 of us was the development of a positive self-image, the use of creative visualization, the transcendence of sex roles, and the use of support groups.

Although some may say that this is not a major conclusion, I choose to disagree. Bear in mind that this book is addressed to gay male managers and executives. One hundred and eighty-eight individuals (94 percent) surveyed have not experienced the stage of Actualization and Manifestation. For those individuals, and for those they are samples of, knowing that the odyssey is possible is a major conclusion. The use of support groups and models were necessary enablers. The 12 (6 percent) of those surveyed who had completed their odyssey are now there as models and encouragers of the other 94 percent of those surveyed.

It has been the experience of the 45 (surveyed and interviewed) regarding the perception of danger and risk, that fear is a perception, not a reality. *Facing the fear, going into it, and coming through it, is the only strategy.* The enablers, role models, and support systems are there to assist one to move from the Reactive Wave (disempowerment) through the "neutral zone" to the Proactive Wave (empowerment). One must trust that the role models and supporters will be there, and they will be! The only other choice is disempowerment.

Recommendations

This study addressed the questions:

- What have gay males experienced as members of straight business organizations?
- Does the model of transition from disempowerment to empowerment, formed from my own experience, hold true for others?
- What enablers operate to permit gay males to continue to move toward empowerment?

It did not address in detail, strategies, mechanisms, or action-steps. Although models were presented, this research was never conceived of as being a "how-to" manual in and of itself. Nevertheless, I see this work as laying the foundation for further studies specifically designed to assist gays to move, step-by-step, through the transition model. This study addresses the questions, "What is happening?" and, "So what?" The question "Now what?" needs further exploration. It is my intent to use this work as a launching pad for a book which focuses on the critical issues of "how to" achieve Actualization and Manifestation.

It is further recommended that future studies address the issue of transcendence of sex-role and sexual-orientation stereotyping in organizations. Some work has been done on sex-role stereotyping of work function, but, to my knowledge, no work has addressed the sexual-orientation stereotyping of work function.

In addition, it is my hope that this study can serve as a base for future studies to address the question: To what extent are the lesbian and gay male's experiences similar or dissimilar? The variable of being a female, especially a lesbian of color, should provide an even more dramatic insight in the field of Organizational Psychology.

It was the intent of this effort to make a significant contribution to the area of gay studies within Organizational Psychology. I believe that what is contained in these pages achieves that goal. Furthermore, the content of this book is based on the belief that each word, theme, and chapter has been presented for the achievement of the highest good for all.

To my fellow gay male executives, I leave you with these words:

Silence = Death
Action = Life

–Act Up

Bibliography

A Course in Miracles. (1976). Glen Ellen, CA: Foundation for Inner Peace.

Adams, J., Hayes, J., and Hapson, B. (1976). *Transition.* London: Martin Robinson.

American Psychological Association. (1975, Jan.). Council Policy Reference Book. Washington, DC, pp. 122-123.

Beckhard, R. and Harris, R. (1977). *Organizational Transitions: Managing Complex Change.* Reading, MA: Addison-Wesley.

Bell, Alan P. and Weinberg, Martin S. (1978). *Homosexuality: A Study of Diversity Among Men and Women.* New York: Simon and Schuster.

Bems, S. (1975). *Androgyny and Mental Health.* Paper presented at the meeting of the American Psychological Association, Chicago, IL.

Bennis, W. G. and Shepard, H. A. (1956). A theory of group development. *Human Relations.* Vol. 9., pp. 415–437.

Berne, E. (1966). *Principles of Group Treatment.* New York: Oxford University Press.

Bion. W. R. (1961). *Experience in Groups.* New York: Basic Books.

Blake, R. and Mouton, J. (1970). The fifth achievement. *The Journal of Applied Behavioral Science.* Vol. 6, No. 4, pp. 413-426.

Block, Peter. (1987). *The Empowered Manager.* San Francisco: Jossey-Bass.

Boswell, John. (1980). *Christianity, Social Tolerance, and Homosexuality.* Chicago: University of Chicago Press.

Bridges, W. (1986). Managing organizational transitions. *Organizational Dynamics.* New York: AMA, *15*, No. 1 (summer), p. 25.

Capra, F. (1982). The turning point: A new vision of reality. *The Futurist, 16*, pp. 22-31.

Carroll, Lewis (1990). *The Annotatated Alice.* Introduction and notes by Martin Gardner. New York: Crown Publisher.

Carse, J. P. (1986). *Finite and Infinite Games*. New York: Free Press.

Carsini, R. (1979). *Current Psychotherapies*. Itasca, IL: Peacock.

Confidential Interviews. References to dates and cities have been omitted to ensure anonymity.

Covey, Stephen R. (1989). *The 7 Habits of Highly Effective People*. New York: Simon and Schuster.

Cramer, Kathryn D. (1990). *Staying on Top When Your World Turns Upside Down*. New York: Viking.

Crew, Louie. (1978). Before Emancipation: Gay Persons as Viewed by Chairpersons in English. In Louie Crew (Ed.), *The Gay Academic*, pp. 3-48. Palm Springs, CA: ETC Publications.

Davidson, S. (1985). *Rock Hudson: His Story*. New York: William Morrow.

Durant, Will. (1961). *The Story of Philosophy*. New York: Simon and Schuster.

Erikson, Eric H. (1959). Identity and the life-cycle. *Psychological Issues*. Vol. 1, pp. 1-171.

Fisher, P. (1978). *The Gay Mystique*. New York: Stein and Day.

Fowler, James W. (1982). *Stages of Faith: The Psychology of Human Development and the Quest for Meaning*. San Francisco: Harper and Row.

Freedman, M. (1975a). Far from illness: Homosexuals may be healthier than straights. *Psychology Today*, (March), pp. 28-32.

Freedman, M. (1975b). *Personal Definition and Psychological Function*. New York: Harper and Row.

Gawain, S. (1982). *Creative Visualization*. New York: Bantam.

Gayle, Rubin. (1984). Thinking Sex, in Carole Vance (Ed.), *Pleasure and Danger: Exploring Female Sexuality*. London: Routledge and Kegan Paul.

Gibb, J. R. and Gibb, L. M. (1955). *Applied Group Dynamics*. Washington, DC: NTL.

Gonsiorek, J. C. (1991). The empirical basis for the demise of the illness models in homosexuality. In J. C. Gonsiorek and J. D. Weinrick (Eds.), *Homosexuality: Research Implications for Public Policy*. Newburg Park, CA: Sage.

Gonsiorek, J. C. (1993). Threat, stress, and adjustment: Mental health and the workplace for gay and lesbian individuals. In L.

Diamont (Ed.), *Homosexuality Issues in the Workplace*. Washington, DC: Taylor and Francis.

Hedgeth, J. M. (1979/1980). Empowerment discrimination law and the rights of gay persons. *Journal of Homosexuality*, 5(1/2), pp. 67-68.

Herman, J. (1983). *La Cage aux Folles*. (Musical). New York: Jerryco Music Company.

Hooker, E. A. (1957). The adjustment of the overt male homosexual. *Journal of Projective Techniques, 21*, pp. 17-31.

I Ching. (1950). (R. Wilhelm, Trans.). New York: Bollingen Foundation, Princeton University Press.

Ingalls, J. D. (1976). *Human Energy*. Reading, MA: Addison-Wesley.

Johnson, Robert A. (1986). *Inner Work*. San Francisco: Harper and Row.

Jung, C. G. (1971). *Collected Works*. Princeton, NJ: Princeton University Press.

Kanter, R. M. and Stein, B. A. (1980). *A Tale of "O."* New York: Harper and Row.

Keen, E. (1970). *Three Forces of Being: Toward an Existential Clinical Psychology*. Englewood Cliffs, NJ: Prentice Hall.

Keen, S. (1983). *The Passionate Life*. New York: Harper and Row.

Kohlberg, L. (1969). Stages and sequence: The cognitive-developmental approach to socialization. In D. S. Goslin (Ed.), *Handbook of Socialization and Research*. Chicago: Rand McNally.

Knutson, D. C. (1979). Job security for gays: Legal aspects. In B. Bergan and R. Leighton (Eds.), *Positively Gay*. Millbrae, CA: Celestial Arts.

Krip, David L. (1989). "Uncommon decency: Pacific Bell responds to AIDS," *Harvard Business Review*. May/June, pp. 140-151.

Kübler-Ross, E. (1969). *On Death and Dying*. New York: Macmillan.

Levine, M. P. (1989). The status of gay men in the workplace. In M. Kimmel and M. Missner (Eds.), *Men's Lives*. New York: Macmillan.

Levine, S. (1979). *A Gradual Awakening*. New York: Anchor.

Levinson, Daniel, Darrow, Charlotte N., Klein, Edward B., Levinson, Maria H., and McKee, Braxton. (1978). *The Seasons of Man's Life*. New York: Knopf.

Machiavelli, Niccolo. (1981). *The Prince*. Translated by George Bull. New York: Penguin Books.

Maslow, A. H. (1986). *Toward a Psychology of Being*. New York: Van Nostrand Reinhold.

Moore, Thomas. (1992). *Care of the Soul*. New York: Harper Collins.

Olson, W. C. (1986). Defeating the enemy: Some guidelines. *Christopher Street, 100*, pp. 8-11.

Painter, Kim (1988). "Many would discriminate over AIDS," *USA Today*. October 13, 1988.

Peck, M. S. (1978). *The Road Less Traveled*. New York: Simon and Schuster.

Peck, M. S. (1987). *The Different Drum*. New York: Simon and Schuster.

Peck, M. S. (1994). *Further Along the Road Less Traveled*. New York: Simon and Schuster.

Plotinus. (1964). *The Essential Plotinus*. (E. O'Brien, Transl.). Indianapolis: Hackett.

Rosenfels, P. (1971). *Homosexuality: The Psychology of the Creative Process*. New York: Libra.

Roth, Nancy L. and Carman, Judith. (1993). Risk perception and HIV legal issues in the workplace. In Louis Diamont (Ed.), *Homosexual Issues in the Workplace*. Washington, DC: Taylor and Francis.

Rothenberg, David. (1979). "Oppression and political disadvantage," *Gayweek*, February 5, 1979, p.19.

Rubin, Gayle. (1984). Thinking sex. In Carole Vance (Ed.), *Pleasure and Danger: Exploring Female Sexuality*, pp. 267-319. London: Routledge and Kegan Paul.

Russo, Vito. (1990). Letter to the editor. *Village Voice*, April 24, 1990, p. 4.

Saghir, Marcel T. and Robins, Eli. (1973). *Male and Female Homosexuality: A Comprehensive Investigation*. Baltimore: Williams and Wilkins.

Sargent, A. G. (Ed.). (1977). *Beyond Sex Roles*. St. Paul, MN: West.

Sargent, A. G. (1983). *The Androgynous Manager*. New York: AMACOM.

Seligman, Martin. (1989). *Learned Optimism*. Westminster, MD: Knopf.

Sheahy, Gail. (1974). *Passages.* New York: Bantam Books.

St. Lawrence, J. S., Husfeldt, B. A., Kelly, J. A, Hood, H. V., and Smith, S. (1990). The stigma of AIDS: Fear of disease and prejudice toward gay men. *Journal of Homosexuality.* 19(3), pp. 85-101.

Tillich, P. (1952). *The Courage to Be.* New Haven, CT: Yale University Press.

Tuckerman, B. W. (1965). Developmental sequence in small groups. *Psychological Bulletin,* Vol. 63, pp. 384-399.

U.S. Department of Labor. (1991). *A Report on the Glass Ceiling Initiative.* Washington, DC: Office of Information and Public Affairs.

Von Franz, Maria. (1979). Unpublished lecture, Panoria Conference. Los Angeles, CA.

Walsh, Roger and Vaughan, Frances. (1993). The art of transcendence: An introduction to common elements of transpersonal practices. *Journal of Transpersonal Psychology,* 25(1), pp. 1-9.

Webster's New Collegiate Dictionary. (1977). Springfield, MA: G&C Merriam Company.

Wilhelm-Buckley, K. and Perkins, D. (1984). *Transforming Work.* Alexandria, VA: Miles River.

Williamson, Marianne. (1992). *A Return to Love.* New York: Harper Collins.

Wilson, P. (1979). Towards a new understanding of the gender of organizations. Unpublished PDE. Union for Experimenting Colleges and Universities, Cincinnati.

Woods, James D. and Lucas, Jay H. (1993). *The Corporate Closet.* New York: The Free Press.

Zoglin, R. (1979). What it's like to be gay in a pin-striped world. In M. P. Levine (Ed.), *Gay Men: The Sociology of Male Homosexuality,* pp. 68-77. New York: Harper and Row.

Index

Gay Model of Transition, Stage III
(anger and conflict) *(continued)*
percentage of gay managers
and executives in, 136,137
Stage IV (depression and
victimization), 39,45,62-63
Stage V (internalization and
transformation), 45,63-70
dealing behaviors in, 68,69
motivators in, 68,69
percentage of gay managers
and executives in, 141
"unveiling" during, 55
Stage VI (actualization and
manifestation), 29-30,45,
70-76,78
meditation and, 79
percentage of gay managers
and executives in, 146
reversion from, 39
strategies, 39
validity of, 142
waves, 38. *See also* Gay Model
of Transition, coactive wave;
proactive wave; reactive
wave
Gay Mystique, The (Fisher), 11-12
Gays, attitudes towards their
homosexuality, 144-145
Glass ceiling
for gays, 60
for women, 5
Goal determination, 68
Golden Gate Business Council,
107-108
Goodstein, David, 138
Greater Washington Business
and Professional Council, 15,
123
Growth, personal, 68,69

Hapson, B., 41
Harassment, of gays, 8
Hawaii, Kahma Healers of, 83

Hayes, J., 41
Hegel, Georg Wilhelm, 55
Helplessness, 58
Heterosexual, definition of, 12-13
Heterosexuality
definition of, 12-13
as positive value, 8
Heterosexual, definition of, 12-13
Heterosexual men
coming out by, 53
homophobic attitudes of, 13-14
stereotypes of, 10-11
Heterosexual paradigm, of
the business community, 10,
12-13,15-16,115
Heuristics, as research method, 4,
120-122,126-127
HIV-positive individuals, 22
Holistic-ecological-systems
perspective, 37
Homophobes, gay-affirmative
responses to, 92-93
Homophobia
AIDS-related, 22-24
of corporate environment, 16,92.
See also Heterosexual
paradigm, of the business
community
of heterosexual men, 13-14
internalized
expressed as gay degradation,
101,103-104
removal of, 79
Homosexual
definition of, 12-13
as medical and pathological term, 4
Homosexuality
as choice, 77-78
definition of, 12-13
equated with femininity, 8,9,10,
11-12,19,145
gays' attitudes toward, 144-145
goodness of, 3,78,83,94
as negative value, 8,9